4 BRS

The French
Bistro
ChAiR

The French Bistro ChAiR

– Maison Drucker –

ALIX DE DIVES
SERGE GLEIZES

PHOTOGRAPHY
JEAN-MARC PALISSE

ABRAMS | NEW YORK

fore word

Patrick Frey

I have known Bruno Dubois, now the director of Drucker, since the age of twenty. He has become a friend. I have deep admiration for his loyalty, sincerity, courage, extreme kindness, and the relationship he has with Mone.

He has worked all his life for his children and his family, holding key positions in various fields, striking a fine balance between family life and professional career.

Like Maison Drucker, which he took the helm of several years ago, we too have a passion for weaving. Our two industries are ultimately complementary. While Drucker produces furniture mainly for outdoors, Pierre Frey designs and produces fabrics for indoor use. Today, these boundaries have been abolished: Drucker furniture is gaining more and more ground indoors, and some of our fabrics are now appearing outside.

Just like Pierre Frey, Drucker is a business with a savoir-faire that is typically French, and very Parisian, which immediately evokes our beautiful capital, our bistros, our café terraces, and something positive and permanent: a *joie de vivre à la française*. I like the little individualistic note of each of its chairs, their lightness, their colors, their design, their craftsmanship, and their timelessness. These are products that have always interested me and that I find truly endearing.

I have deep respect for what my friend Bruno has done with Drucker, combining technical expertise and custom design without ever getting carried away by a demand for quantity. He has made it a brand in his image: chic and authentic.

Colbert armchair, basic caning (black, ivory) from Drucker,
and rolls of Mani jacquard fabric (charcoal black, curry yellow) from Pierre Frey.

SUMMARY

Introduction

It is a phenomenon in itself. It is discreet yet very visible, light, and resistant to everything, most of all to the passage of time. During the course of a little over a century, the Drucker chair has been like a beautiful lady who has not aged in the slightest. Although now found on terraces around the world, it is most intimately linked to the history of Parisian cafés: Café de Flore, Les Deux Magots, Brasserie Lipp, the Rhumerie... just to talk about Boulevard Saint-Germain. With its original, inventive, colorful and chic caning, its slightly exotic aspect and its artisanal charm, it is the Parisian bistro chair *par excellence*. The one that presides on a café terrace, that invites you to enjoy the sunshine, to read your newspaper, to set down your shopping bag. The one to save for the person who'll be joining you. It might be the leading subject of an article, on the cover of a book or feature in fashion shoots. It is part of a scenery, a story, a romance. And even those who don't know its origin, its method of manufacture, its secrets or its history, still know the Drucker chair, and have for over a century. This includes French and foreign designers. Here lies its mystery and charm; in its allure, its resonance, and its poetry.

RATTAN, *an* Ode *to* NaTuRe

※

atural, delicate, light, flexible, susceptible to all imaginable aesthetic twists to become a chair, armchair, canapé, cabinet, table or lamp, the rattan vine, sometimes growing over two hundred meters, is a plant fiber of countless virtues. It is ecological, and has low sensitivity to temperature changes since it grows in tropical countries with a hot climate alternating dry and wet seasons. And it is resistant, due to its siliceous membrane that gives it natural protection. It can also be worked just as it is, without undergoing any, or very little, transformation. Of course, compared to materials like wood, stone or metal that are also used to make furniture, rattan seems fragile, but only in appearance. And for proof: the rattan that grows in the Malay Archipelago of the Moluccas, the Sunda Islands, the plains of the Mekong Delta and Vietnam is used to make cables and ropes for ships!

The many varieties of this plant with its grayish thorn-covered trunk offer qualities appreciated since time immemorial for shaping frames and decorative elements. Rattan vines are worked raw, spliced or debarked, according to well-known and almost immutable processes.

The raw vine undergoes a treatment, and a very light one at that, which is simply to remove the leaves and thorns from the stem. Packaged in the three- or four-meter rods of different diameters, it retains its natural protection and will be selected for the creation of seat frames and manufactured objects. Its color, ranging from yellow to green, varies by species.

During the splicing operation, the vine is split into thin strips, which are rounded on one side and flat on the other. These natural strips of a beautiful ecru color are what are used for caning. The central part of the vine, the rattan marrow, will meanwhile be sanded and calibrated through a machine. Rendered perfectly cylindrical, the rattan marrow is the basis of all traditional weaving.

Debarking involves "peeling" the canes with a machine to remove the skin that stiffens them. The poles thus obtained are easier to work with. Sensitive to moisture, this rattan is used mainly for the production of seats and interior furnishings.

Plants producing rattan, known as rattan palms, including the iconic species *Calamus rotang*, are part of the Calamus family. They are wild palms endemic in Asian tropical forests. A first category of rattan, of a beautiful brown color, comes mainly from Malacca in Malaysia, Sumatra, Sulawesi and Borneo in Indonesia, the Philippines and Vietnam. It is increasingly difficult today to procure this rattan, in a context where the fight against excessive deforestation is accompanied by the implementation of sustainable environmental and economic policies. Growing in aquatic conditions, Malacca rattan is not sensitive to moisture, and its siliceous texture makes it resistant to impact.

A second category of light-colored rattan, from Manila, the tropical forests of Indonesia and Vietnam, comes from a thin-stemmed palm tree that grows in the shade of trees in lush forests, on the edge of rice fields and near waterways. Fast growing, this palm can produce vines up to two hundred meters long.

In total, there are more than two hundred varieties of rattan, including Java bamboo, cane rattan, rope rattan, and rattan of Manau, Tohiti, Sarawak, Sampit and Pasir. They come in a range of colors, from light to brown. For example, the rattan produced from the dragon's blood palm has a beautiful natural brown color. This plant's fruit is covered with dark red "dragon's blood" resin, commonly used as a pigment and integrated in traditional pharmacopoeia. More prosaically, rattan can be dyed brown with a preparation of pork fat and coconut oil, or even by dipping it into an oil bath. Functional and aesthetic, Malacca and Manila rattan were adopted early on by the fashion industry, to make canes, bag handles, bins, baskets, umbrellas and parasols. It also enjoyed widespread use in decoration and furniture, especially for furniture pieces designed to decorate the interior gardens of houses and bourgeois apartments.

Previous double page, left: light Manila rattan cane; right: dark rattan cane – here lathed – from Malacca.
A sure and easy way to identify them by color? Vanilla = Manila, and chocolate = Malacca!
Opposite: a reissue of an iconic piece of Drucker furniture, the *Confortable* three-seat bench. Classic herringbone caning of natural fibers.

Since the eighteenth century, the manner of harvesting wild rattan has slightly changed: the vines are cut with machetes in their natural environment, and then assembled into bundles and transported on men's backs. Next they are stripped of their bark and thorns, then washed, dried, sorted and stored before being shipped to Europe.

Indonesia banned the export of raw rattan in 1986 to save its forests, and then reinforced this measure in 2012 with a trade embargo. However, it still remains the largest rattan producer in the world. Cambodia, Vietnam, West and Central Africa, India and South America have in turn become notable exporters. They also have their production supervised by international associations advocating sustainable growing and techniques meeting environmental criteria. Thus, the International Network for Bamboo and Rattan (INBAR) has implemented a sustainable development program including the creation of nurseries, maintenance of seedlings and crop management. In fact, the rattan palms specific to tropical Asian ecosystems could be planted elsewhere and thus used to help stop soil erosion, restore soil fertility, drain the soil or even bring water towards the surface where needed. The benefits of rattan cultivation for the environment are multiple and undeniable. Yet, in competition for the past thirty years with synthetic materials, rattan is being used less and less for decoration, even though the new products, as easy to work with as natural fiber, still do not boast all its qualities nor offer such an incredible sheen.

It is clear, however, that after experiencing a sharp decline, demand for rattan is rising again. No doubt, this is a sign of our time that, despite its fondness for rampant consumption, still advocates ecological responsibility and demonstrates a renewed interest in natural products.

RATTAN,
a Timeless Rendez-vous

Rattan was born in Antiquity and appeared in the furniture of certain Egyptian tombs, but it was really lionized in the eighteenth century and during the French Second Empire. In the nineteenth and twentieth century, it invaded public spaces, appearing in all the salons and decorative magazines of the period, before conquering the world of radical design, without ever sinking into coldness or losing its poetry.

With its rattan frame dressed in a *weave of bright colors*, the Drucker chair has become, in a little over a century, a *Parisian icon*. It represents a pinnacle of *comfort, aesthetics, lightness* and *strength*, that is at once playful, cheerful and bright. It has an innate *elegance* worthy of the capital, tinged with the flavor of faraway lands. A bit like those antique porcelains or family furnishings that have been passed down from generation to generation, things you wouldn't part with for the world since they carry the sweet *melody of memories*. Each creation by Drucker is *timeless*, even more so given that custom design has been an integral part of the company's history since its first workshop was founded in 1885.

F*re*N*ch*
HISTORY
of Rattan

Registered in the Drucker archives, the *Capucine* model of the late 19th / early 20th century, one of the oldest of the company, originally made for the Café de la Paix. Exceptional double-star caning of natural fibers.

it is touching to note that, rattan was already used in Antiquity for the frame of some seats found in Egyptian tombs. However, the true revival of rattan work began in the eighteenth century, before the French Second Empire exalted it with unprecedented enthusiasm. Coming from distant lands, rattan was a sign of the era's new infatuation with the Orient and the Far East. Another contributing factor in its success was its very reasonable cost: first of all, the low cost of Malaysian, Indian and Filipino labor to harvest the rattan canes in the jungle, and then the very affordable import costs. The primary exporting country, Indonesia, was part of the Dutch East Indies at the time, and sheaves of rattan were used to stabilize the goods in the holds of ships bound for Amsterdam.

For Europe, the eighteenth century was a time of colonial expansion and major maritime trade. Portugal and Spain had already founded vast colonial empires and the Netherlands, England and France sent their India Company vessels to this mysterious and distant Asia to fetch unknown treasures. Merchants returned with spices, certainly, but also with rattan or wicker, a hardy plant fiber used in India and Indonesia to make ropes and rigging, as well as other functional and decorative objects. Commercialized in Europe, the rattan lengths were sliced into 2-mm-wide strips to make the seats and backs of chairs. The creation of a cane chair was thus a dual process: beginning with the carpenter who made the wooden frame, followed by the cane worker who completed the piece. This was the advent of "*cannage à la française*," a technique that is still practiced today.

With such cane work, the armchairs under the French Regency and the reign of Louis XV advocated a certain return to simplicity, a form of rebellion against the splendor of the previous century. Inspired by the naturalistic style in vogue at the time and the exotic themes culled from travels around the world, upholstery fabrics were readily being replaced by inventive and sophisticated cane weaves. The French Regency style set the tone for this decorative manner as shown in 1722 when the inventory of the furniture of Versailles, noted for the first time the presence of seats, cabriolets, armchairs and wing chairs... in cane. After an interruption during the Revolution, furniture caned with rattan strips reentered interiors. The mid-nineteenth century, however, is when the expansion of trade and maritime transport facilitated the importing of the famous vegetable fiber. The use of rattan cane to structure furniture developed between 1830 and 1850. At that time, decorative tastes were again marked by colonial conquests in Asia—in Tonkin, Annam and Cambodia.

In the nineteenth century, rattan factories craftsmen recruited craftsmen in the fields of basketry. The profession of rattan caner became established, and workshops began to multiply throughout France. Two aesthetic forms emerged: a colonial style that was a pastiche of rattan furniture manufactured in the Far East and imported by Dutch and English companies, and a bourgeois style that was an expression of a decorative formalism and a craft that would be perpetuated until the 1920s. Regardless of trend or construction, rattan furniture decorated winter gardens and, in fine weather, terraces and outdoors. It also reached both the most refined and the simplest interiors. Creations abounded: chaises longues, easy chairs, love seats, crapaud chairs, window boxes, dressers, sewing tables, benches, drawers, canapés... sophisticated weaving, a plethora of colors, new shapes... variations bursting with imagination, creativity and poetry.

Opposite: a symphony of contemporary models, from the end of the 19th century to the beginning of the 21st, of which some reissued by Drucker. From top to bottom and left to right: *Republica* chair back (2015), *Royal Évian* armchair (1890), *Eugénie* armchair (1915), *Rousseau* armchair (1920), *Saint-Jacques* armchair (1950), *Crapaud* armchair (1900), and *Buci* chair (1930). The ensemble has been produced in Manila rattan, with natural fibers.
Above: a model taken from the archives, the *Montgolfier* bench, created for Michel Debré when he was in the government, between 1959 and 1973.

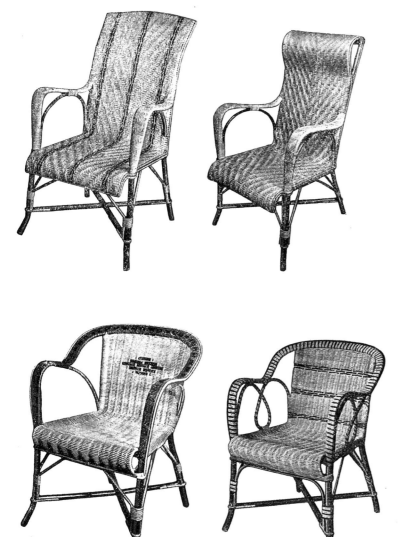

During the Second Empire, Empress Eugénie, who was passionate about fashion and the decorative arts of the previous century, revived a taste for luxury crafts, for lace and silk fabrics, passementarie. This of course stimulated the art of furnishing and therefore the art of rattan. It would invade the finest salons under the Second Empire. A few decades later, it would take on the forms of Art Nouveau and Art Déco. This aesthetic current also appealed to Princess Mathilde, daughter of Jérôme Bonaparte, who would popularize the trend by decorating her luxurious winter gardens with chairs, armchairs, tables and benches in cleverly wrought rattan imbued with exotic elegance. Italy, the cradle of all arts, experienced the same enthusiasm with Chiavari chairs, which had been designed at the dawn of the century and were widely disseminated at that time. In fact, most of the major courts of Europe adopted these chairs, which were lightweight and robust, and could be found at the many receptions given by Empress Eugénie.

FROM USUAL CREATIONS TO SPECIAL ORDERS

This was the highly dynamic context in which Drucker was founded. It opened its first workshop in 1885 and played a key role in the success of rattan from the start. Weathering two wars, oil crises, the vagaries of fashion and the upheavals of the twentieth century, Drucker remains to this day the reference in the field.

The early twentieth century was a heyday for the craftsman who, as both artist and manufacturer, designed and built with the same creative élan. The right of exclusivity did not exist. The idea of legal protection for a registered design was not considered, and work in rattan did not enjoy any special status. The rattan worker learned his skills on the job, and copying was never considered

Left: the Drucker workshops in Béthisy-Saint-Martin (Oise), in the 1940s.
Right: among the winter garden models from the beginning of the 20th century, the *Rodin* armchair. Classic diadem caning (jade green, brick, putty) with large brick-red piping.

plagiarism because new models were often enhanced versions of previous ones. While some creations presented today in museums were devised for Le Printemps department store or created for military sanatoriums, such as wheelchairs or chaises longues, the bulk of the collection was produced for terraces, gardens, verandas, and summer dining rooms, just like today. Hard wearing, rattan was a great source of creative richness, ensuring the fantasy, variety of colors and shapes required to make furniture that could be at once refined, affordable, functional and intended for everyday use. It was a kind of foreshadowing of the current trend in decoration toward abolishing the boundaries between the outside and inside, for furniture that was simple, durable and exotic. In this way, Drucker honored the prestigious orders of the grand hotels of the era, such as the Hôtel Royal in Evian, or the Hôtel Continental in Paris, furnished with chairs created in five different chromatic tones. And while competing companies grew in number, Drucker remained the leader. In Paris, in 1920, the La Samaritaine and Bazar de l'Hôtel-de-Ville department stores devoted an entire section to rattan, and especially Drucker furniture, with chairs suspended from the ceiling. Le Printemps and Les Trois-Quartiers also asked the manufacturers to propose exclusive creations for their stores. During the Belle Époque, the rattan caned chair gained widespread popularity, causing production to soar. The rattan chair took the sidewalk bistros by storm, and made them its permanent home.

Previous double page,
left: the curve of the backs is held in place by metal clamps to ensure a final curvature; right the *Grenelle* armchair, with Malacca cane base and simple caning (grey, white).
Left: chaise longue, early 20th century, Drucker archives, with adjustable backrest, and removable armrests and footrests.
Right: in stock, stack of *Bastille* chairs in Malacca rattan.
Classic caning (grey-white).

BASKETRY, MEDIEVAL ARTISTIC CRAFTSMANSHIP

Dating from the Neolithic Period in Mesopotamia, plant fiber weaving techniques can be traced much further back than the fashion for rattan. A guild of seat weavers has existed in France since the Middle Ages. The tradition of weaving, and then rattan work in the region of Fayl-Billot in the southern Haute-Marne, originated in the Hermitage of St. Peregrine. Around 1670, one of the monks began to teach the local villagers how to weave wicker baskets and other containers to revive the local economy. This approach was exactly what Colbert was pursuing at the same period, during the reign of Louis XIV, to encourage the development of crafts and create or revitalize French industry and manufacturers battered by the wars. Even if weaving is considered an outdated activity today, it was one of the main economic activities along with agriculture in the Haute-Marne department during the nineteenth and twentieth centuries. The workforce was specialized primarily in Fayl-Billot, which in 1905 became the site of the *École Nationale d'Osiériculture et de Vannerie*. The growth of this activity was therefore largely due to the expansion of new communication and distribution networks, particularly the railway, as well as a redistribution of land that promoted willow farming, and finally, the presence of the essential workforce of craftsmen who enjoyed regular employment and found gratification in the transmission of fine artisanal values. Production diversified and, besides shopping baskets, came to include grape baskets, bird cages, cheese panniers, banneton baskets for bakers, other baskets for butchers, pieces for the office, and now articles of contemporary design.

Opposite: *lunti* or *loonty* creepers – a fine and flexible variety of rattan – are used as strengtheners and ties to edge and reinforce the frames in Malacca and Manila rattan.

EMBRACING AUTHENTICITY

Lightweight and elegant, the rattan chair could be customized and adapted in endless ways for greater comfort and grace. It was virtually indestructible, as well as highly practical since it could be stacked and moved with ease.

Already found in public spaces around the world, on the terraces of hotels and cafés, in bathing and spa facilities, tea rooms, reception areas, art salons, the dining rooms of big passenger ships, on the Lido beaches in Venice, and in the cabins of the first planes between England and France, rattan furniture enjoyed a fantastic promotional campaign in the 1950s. It featured in major art and furniture magazines, such as *Art & Décoration, Maison et jardin, Maison française*, and took center stage at every major professional event, such as the *Salon du Meuble, Salon des Arts Ménagers, Salon des Artistes Décorateurs de Paris*, and other exhibitions in Lyon, Marseille, Strasbourg, and Lille. These sophisticated creations were inspired by the clean lines of the Art Déco movement. Seats and chair backs were mainly woven or caned, or created in openwork wicker —with lower manufacturing costs—, initiating a style that predominated throughout the sixties. The major interior designers also became interested in rattan, and thus played a part in its renewal. These included

Louis Sognot, a protagonist of cubism and the modern movement, Joseph-André Motte, Robert Charlot, Baillon, Gallot, and Lina Zervudachi. Certain stools, small tables, tables and fixtures made of rattan created by the Roche firm dressed the windows of Christian Dior and Marcel Rochas. Decorators designed furniture with clean lines, worked in yellow Manila rattan, and increasingly with metal frames. These tubular structures were easily stacked for easy storage. The only snag was that vegetable fiber was increasingly being replaced by nylon or other synthetic materials, the major revolution of these decades. The taste for authenticity and natural fiber returned when fashion once more honored salons and verandas that were never more comfortable and beautiful to look at than when furnished with rattan creations. There was the same craze for rattan veneer used to finish the structures of cabinets, chests and dressers, or for those rattan fabrics imported from Asia used to decorate the wooden furniture frames. Rattan was definitely ennobled, and widely publicized at the birth of Princess Caroline of Monaco in 1957, since her cradle was created by the Maugrion company in Bayeux.

In the late 1970s, to cope with competition from the Philippines and Thailand, as well as industrial manufacturing techniques, the manufacturers of Fayl-Billot in Haute-Marne, including Maison Petitot, later Château Frères, Maison Pernot, Maison Quevy, and Maison Breuillot, endeavored to give rattan furniture a youthful makeover.

In this period of questions and doubt, Drucker continued to forge ahead. Its activity would remain strong, with a constant concern for quality that still remains today. Certain Drucker models from this period, as timeless as ever, have recently been reissued.

RATTAN AND THE DESIGN WORLD

While Danish designer Nanna Ditzel already showed interest in wicker in the 1950s with her chair and design of the *Basket* chair for the Spanish company Kettal, large retailers benefited from the commercial success of rattan furniture that followed. The first creations appeared in the 1973–1974 Prisunic catalog. The chain of Habitat stores followed the movement that same year in its first French shop—located at the foot of the Montparnasse Tower in Paris—with tubular cantilever *Vadina* wicker chairs and armchairs. In association with Drucker, the store Le Cèdre Rouge launched its own line, just like Grange and Roche Bobois. In 2002, rattan furniture, or at least its reinterpretation, was once more revived by another big Swedish name, IKEA, for whom Thomas Sandell, Mats Theselius, Monika Mudler and James Irvine designed the PS collection with chairs of hand-woven plastic perfectly imitating natural rattan. In 2007, the Brazilian brothers Fernando and Humberto Campana designed the *TransPlastic* seats using Brazilian *apuí* vegetable fiber, similar to rattan. In 2011, the Designboom collective, charmed by the material, designed rattan furniture and had it produced by artisans on the banks of the Mekong. Back in Europe, Spanish designer Jaime Hayon also became interested in rattan, as did Romeo Sozzi, creator and artistic director of the Italian furniture firm Promemoria, which combines leather, velvet, bronze and precious woods in an Haute Couture spirit, notably for the *Oliveto* canapé as well as a line of outdoor furniture. With his *Phoenix*, a three-wheeled car built around a biodegradable body of bamboo and rattan, Filipino designer Kenneth Cobonpue draws close to one of the most important causes of the day, saving the planet, as part of an environmentally responsible vision for the management of plantations and the development of fair trade.

Vintage Side

While rattan remains a material frequently used to create everyday furniture that is affordable, ecological and aesthetic, some of the rarer creations of the nineteenth century have become much sought after. This idea is championed by the antique dealer Laurence Vauclair, who specializes in barbotine and majolica in her boutique on Rue de Beaune in Paris and at *Aidjolate Antiquités* in the Paul Bert market Porte de Clignancourt. She features exclusive finely worked and poetic winter garden furniture pieces from the nineteenth and twentieth centuries, some signed Perret & Vibert, which she willingly lends to decorate the windows of great fashion houses, or to filmmakers for movie sets. In their superb *British Gallery* on Rue de l'Université in Paris, Philippe and Christine Roux share the same passion, exhibiting along with English furniture from the eighteenth and nineteenth centuries, chairs, sofas and side tables in rattan from the nineteenth century, as well as those by Madeleine Castaing, the great decorator of the postwar years. However, it is the rattan furniture of the fifties that Muriel Eveillé and Isabelle Gagnebet uphold at *L'Atelier du Petit Parc* located on Allée Baco in Nantes, closer to what is being done today in contemporary art (see pictures on these pages).

Drucker

History Made to Measure

although the Drucker chair is a typically French creation, the history of this beautiful family saga began in Poland, when the Russian Empire had become terribly repressive in the wake of the January 1863 uprising. The ensuing climate of terror and intolerance would cause a mass exodus, reinforced by the strong draw of a Western Europe in the throes of industrialization. Between 1870 and 1914, around three and a half million Poles, a third of which were Jews, left their homeland. Ten thousand Poles would settle in France in the northern mining region.

This was the dramatic context into which Louis Drucker was born in Poland in 1864 and that would cause his family to move to France, settling first in Alsace, then in Paris. The horror of persecution was now behind them, but this new life was still not the easiest for expatriates. Appreciating the chance to live in a country at peace, the Drucker family always put on a brave face through the hard time and took great pains to honor the nation that had welcomed them. Louis was raised with the essential values of honesty, hard work and respect. Between 1884 and 1886, when he was in his early twenties, he learned the craft of working rattan in Lyon at the Maison Martiné, and then completed his training by learning bamboo work. Very quickly, the young craftsman wanted to break out on his own and create his company, especially as he had talent and imagination, and his pieces had attracted attention. In 1885, after acquiring French nationality, Louis Drucker and an apprentice of Maison Martiné, M. Leredde, opened a tiny workshop of twenty-four square meters at 180 Rue des Pyrénées, in the 20th arrondissement of Paris. The quality of Leredde & Drucker creations garnered numerous awards: a medal at the *Exposition Internationale d'Hygiène, Sauvetage, Secours Publics, Arts Industriels* in 1904, silver and gilt medals from the Brussels World's Fair in 1910, as well as a bronze medal awarded by King Albert I of Belgium in person. Encouraged by this success, they expanded the workshop until it occupied the entire first floor of the building.

FROM NATURAL FIBER TO COLOR

After the Great War, M. Leredde left the company and Louis Drucker took over the entire business. Despite the difficulties inherent in the post-war years, production still grew. As in all family businesses of the time, Louis also had his wife and children involved. This did not displease Mme Drucker: she had artistic flair and painted the sketch boards in watercolor. Giving a unique tone to each creation, she exerted a strong influence on the company's collections. The first catalog was launched in 1919. Orders poured in, but the workshop on Rue des Pyrénées was no longer sufficient to meet demand. A move was necessary: while the offices remained in Paris, production was transferred to Béthisy-Saint-Martin, in the Oise region, not far from Crépy-en-Valois, where the manufacturer of Maxime Clair rattan furniture was already located. Although the region benefitted from a large workforce, no experienced wicker workers came knocking on the Drucker company's door. Louis Drucker would have to train his craftsmen himself to increase production. Rattan was used mainly for the manufacture of garden furniture, however, so rattan workers were essentially seasonal, and busy at their task in spring and summer. They would thus spend sunny days furniture caning, working up to seventy-two hours a week, while the rest of the year, in the fall and early winter, they would lend their strength to harvesting sugar beet. The Picardy plains were already then, and still are today, the primary sugar-producing region of France and all of Europe.

In the 1920s, the rattan industry reached its peak. New factories opened in the provinces and in Paris, and new names were gaining recognition, such as Grock and Gatti, direct competitors

Ameublement en rotin

DRUCKER

MAISON FONDÉE EN 1885

MANUFACTURE DE MEUBLES EN ROTIN
L. DRUCKER
180, Rue des Pyrénées -:- PARIS - XXᵉ

TÉLÉPHONE : ROQUETTE 34-10   Métro : GAMBETTA   R. C. Seine 139.808

CHAISES & FAUTEUILS EN ROTIN POUR CAFÉS, CASINOS, ÉTABLISSEMENTS PUBLIC

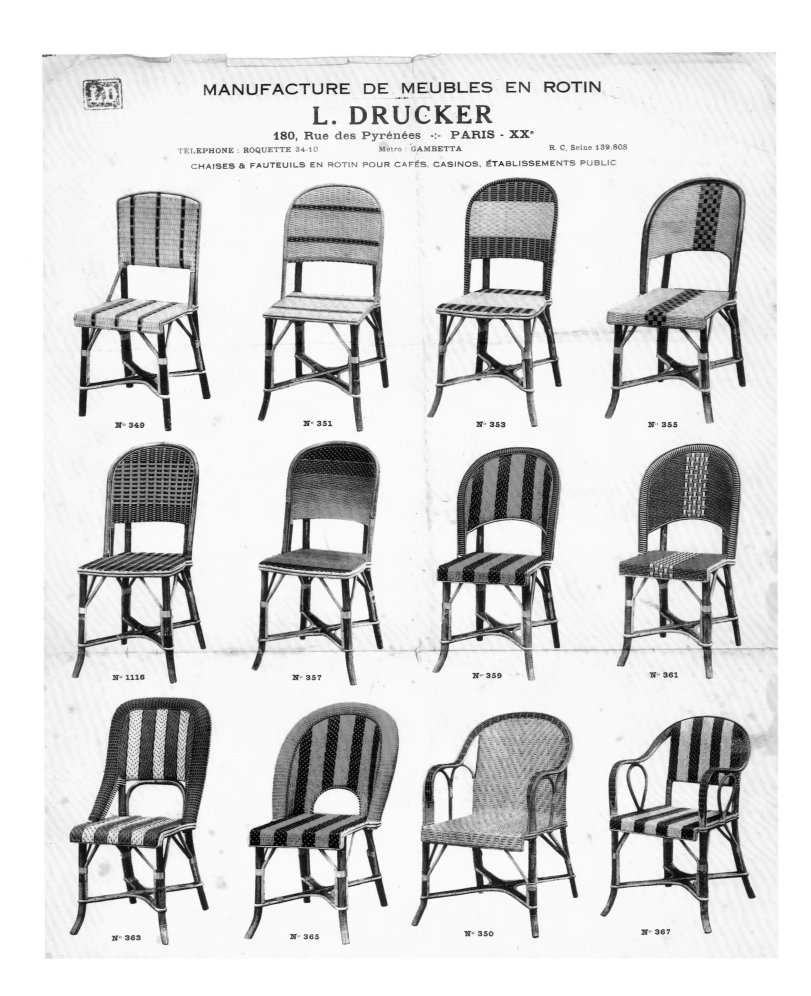

Nº 349   Nº 351   Nº 353   Nº 355

Nº 1116   Nº 357   Nº 359   Nº 361

Nº 363   Nº 365   Nº 350   Nº 367

Nº 1116   Nº 357   Nº 359   Nº 361

Nº 363   Nº 365   Nº 350   Nº 367

Nº 369   Nº 371   Nº 373   Nº 375

PHOTOTYPIE
22, RUE PAUL BERT

to Drucker. At Fayl-Billot, the hub of the Haute-Marne wicker-work industry, rattan tended to replace willow in the workshops. This was the choice that the Raguet manufactories demonstrated with success when they presented their creations at the prestigious *Exposition Internationale des Arts Décoratifs et Industriels Modernes* of 1925, in Paris, before making a sensation with their famous piece of entrance furniture created for the music hall star Mistinguett. Several companies were also created in Fayl-Billot: Petitot (whose founder came from wickerwork) and Minot in 1920, followed by Roberty in 1926. Though Drucker was not the only company specializing in rattan work, it stood out by its consistently high quality and its taste for color, essential to the diversification and sophistication of its models and caning techniques. It knew how to take advantage of the wide color range proposed by the company importing raw rattan, which had developed a process for staining rattan in 1920. Moreover, its caning patterns were created by real artists, mostly women, who combined technical prowess and aesthetic talent. These were strengths that the company built upon and still count among its finest qualities today.

At Drucker, quality was a constant concern. Year after year, the company continued to receive awards of excellence: two bronze medals, four silvers, two gilts, and five golds.

The richness of its catalogs and the significant increase in customers testified at this time to the company's vitality. In the 1920s, Drucker rattan furniture, until then primarily intended for outdoor spaces, was increasingly moving indoors. Rattan plant fiber, already well suited to the manufacture of chairs and tables, became a favorite material for designing other furniture pieces, from lamp stands, ceiling lights, table lamps, mirrors, magazine holders, umbrella stands, footstools and, pouffes to shelves, stands, sewing boxes, bookcases, screens, and headboards. All these innovations could be found in Paris, Lyon, Lille, Brussels, London, Amsterdam, and even the United States and beyond. Indeed, the new furniture could often be dismantled, stacked, packed and shipped to the end of the world. Britain, Latin America and North America thus became the main rattan furniture importers.

In the period from 1900 to 1930, rattan furniture became a must in the field of furnishing, only to be hit hard by the crash of 1929. The rattan firms then entered a downturn marked by the bankruptcy of large factories, like Raguet in 1934, while also suffering raw material shortages. Drucker, however, was resilient. Ever more creative and enterprising, it would be one of the sector's few survivors on the eve of World War II. It was the company that produced 80% of rattan furniture on the market at the time.

3093 VICTORIA

3021 WAGRAM

3416 CAPUCINE

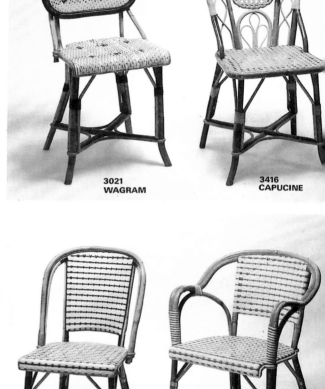

3012 MARLY

3013 FOUQUET'S

3113 TRIANON

2900

3900

7617 VILLAGE

4100

4101

01
08
05
09
10
01
03
09
02
09
09

7618 TABOURET

Diversified production

In 1946, Louis Drucker passed the reins of the firm onto his son Maurice, who decided to concentrate all of its activities in the Oise at Béthisy-Saint-Martin: administration, design and manufacturing. The company now occupied an area of three thousand square meters, and production was reorganized and streamlined to achieve a consistently high level of quality. Its catalog was now filled with living room furniture in Manila rattan or Malacca cane, terrace furniture in rattan and nylon with legs in rattan or metal, lights and other pieces that would forge its reputation and remain highly popular, such as sun loungers and outdoor armchairs in rattan strips or core. Around 1960, the innovation of plastic then brought extra robustness along with a new range of colors.

In 1969, the Drucker catalog offered major stores two hundred models of tables, chairs, armchairs, beds, side tables, night tables and coat hooks. These flagship products were mainly custom made. The client was thus able to choose the form, the weave and the colors. The popularity of rattan owed much to the comfort it provided, its timelessness, and the fact that each chair, for example, adapted to the existing furniture without creating a decorative clash. And if the lucky owners replaced their chairs on average every ten years, it was not so much a matter of wear as being won over by the renewed collections and the rich color palette that had become the signature of Drucker. Alongside the classic silhouettes of armchairs, chairs, stools and side tables, there were also more sophisticated designs like the S-shaped confidants with or without armrests, chaise longues, love seats, and crapaud armchairs: a whole collection of furniture now anchored in the collective memory, representing both a patrimonial savoir-faire and the object of popular culture. The fashion of rattan then gradually began to leave the home to take over the café terraces. The rattan chair became popular with Parisian brasseries for its aesthetic qualities, its lightness, its stackable practicality, its robustness and its weather resistance. The Drucker factory began to receive orders for custom creations. These were designed as visual representations of each establishment's distinctive style, as well as testifying to the refined taste and the dedication to quality of the owners. Each model naturally took the name of its place of residence, such as the *La Coupole* chair, featuring a cane pattern of small cabochons, as well as the *Café de la Paix*, *Drouant*, *Pré Catelan*, and *Fouquet's* chairs.

Left: 1. Piles of pattern and color samples in Rilsan;
2. *Bastille* chair with Versailles caning (white, azure, gold);
3. *Tric-Trac* pedestal, classic caning (ivory, jade green);
4. Classic caning of the *Haussmann* armchair (tobacco, brown, brick).
Right page: *Musée* chair in natural Manila rattan, diamond pattern, ties in black Raucord. And a pair of *Neuilly* chairs with Wagram caning (black, navy blue and aluminum, fuchsia).

Alain Drucker, son of Maurice, represented the third generation of the company. An engineering graduate, he worked with his father on design and creation, without overlooking the manual tradition of the craft, for which he had just as much passion. It was not unusual to find him sitting next to a craftsman, demonstrating a technique of bending or braiding, or discussing how to fix a problem in the manufacturing process. Alain Drucker would work for twenty-four years in the shadow of his father, who did not share his vision for the company and refused to cede his place. Maurice Drucker finally left the company in 1972, and then passed away five years later at the age of seventy-nine. Despite his attachment to the family business, Alain sold it the same year as his father's death. He carefully preserved the company archives, which form an impressive collection of rattan furniture catalogs dating back to 1900.

René-Michel Manseville bought the company in 1979 and created the brand Maison Drucker®. He focused its activity on chairs and armchairs designed for Parisian cafés and brasseries, and developed exports, particularly to the United States. The reputation of these chairs was such that it was not uncommon to simply call a bistro chair by the name of a "Drucker chair"! It would nevertheless be simplifying things to consider it exclusively reserved for the public and professional domain, since individuals continued to adopt it. In 1991, however, the gloomy economic situation in the aftermath of the Gulf War was accompanied by a fall in production. Drucker then entered a difficult period that would last for nearly twenty years, until its bankruptcy reorganization in 2005.

Renaissance

Having previously worked in the industrial sector, Bruno Dubois discovered the story of this legendary chair, and immediately fell under its spell. In January 2006, he bought the company he now runs with his wife Mone.

The reconstruction work encompassed all areas. It would span a good three years. A new website was created presenting unique pieces as well as models from the past. Renowned designers were associated with the creation of new pieces and the updating of pieces from previous collections. Catalogs were published, revealing even more colorful creations, with increasingly bold and innovative weaves. They would be distributed in the world of interior design and at the *Maison & Objet* home show, where the new owner of Maison Drucker met decorators from all around the world.

Manufacturing in the Gilocourt workshop was also revised, reorganized and developed. This approach was proved all the more necessary in 2011, when Indonesia, which supplied 80% of world rattan, decreed a total embargo on the export of raw rattan to focus its activities more on fairer trade. Attentive to the message, Drucker established a workshop in Indonesia to prepare the frames of the chairs, which were then assembled and completed in France. With its know-how in weaving on metal frames, this workshop harmoniously complemented the manufacturing in Gilocourt. This development led to increased sales of over 20% in 2014 and 30% in 2015. Growth was very dynamic in the French market, but also concerned exports, which jumped from 5% in 2006 to over 60% in 2015. Drucker is thus gaining market share in countries where French products are sought out and

Right page: *Bastille* chair with diadem caning (red, brick, water green, gold): "disheveled" back seen from behind while being woven.

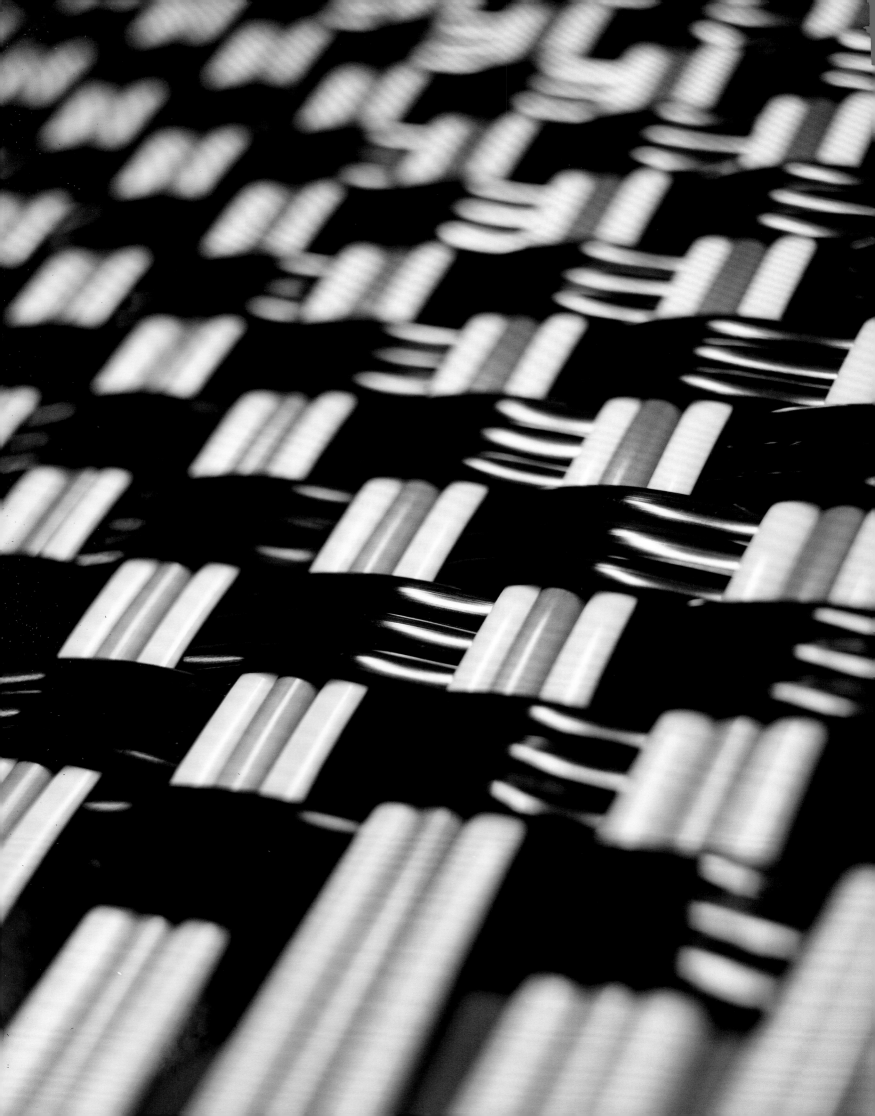

where the image of Paris is strong, such as the United States, United Kingdom, Spain, Germany, Switzerland, Austria and Belgium. Outside Europe and North America, this includes Australia, Japan, New Zealand, Chile, Peru, Bolivia, and many others.

"Abroad, it is simply known as the *'French bistro chair,'* Bruno Dubois revealed to *Ephémère* magazine with regards to the Drucker chair. Because, more than ever, Drucker is the preeminent name for the Parisian bistro chair *par excellence*. The *Seine* model is now found on the terraces of Café de Flore in Paris, just as it is at Les Vapeurs restaurant in Trouville. The *Parnasse* model, with its magnificent weaving in white, petrol blue and burgundy, takes pride of place at Café Rey and Café Français at the Place de la Bastille in Paris, while the chairs of the *Arc-en-ciel* collection furnish the cafés and restaurants of Étretat. Some of the world's most luxurious hotels have also fallen for Drucker furniture, such as the Hôtel Prince de Galles in Paris, which has equipped its interior gardens and terraces with *Trèfle*, *Luxembourg*, *Bastille*, *Auteuil* and *Alesia* chairs and armchairs. The Chateau Marmont Hotel in Los Angeles, Les Deux Magots in Qatar, the Brasseries Georges in Brussels, Gerlóczy restaurant in Budapest, Café Europa in Copenhagen and Marion brewery in Miami are just a few of its other prestigious clients.

At the beginning of the third millennium, the workshops are still based in the Oise, and everything is still handmade, perpetuating the tradition of the company since its founding in 1885. For nearly a century, the pieces proposed, whether "custom" or "ready-to-wear," are still high-end, precise and fascinating works of craftsmanship. One hundred and thirty years of expertise are now put towards a great renewal of forms, redefined and re-orchestrated by colorist Amandine Gallienne who joined the company eight years ago. Renewal of materials too, with the arrival of Rilsan, a polyamide made from castor oil and used for caning, offering even greater resistance to temperature variations, weathering and impacts.

Since 2006, the company has given pride of place to the creations of leading designers and interior designers such as Andrée and Olivia Putman, Jacques Grange, India Mahdavi, François Champsaur, Philippe Starck for Hôtel Royal Monceau, Dorothy Boissier and Patrick Gilles for very upscale restaurants in the United States, Christian Biecher for all Fauchon stores, on Place de la Madeleine in Paris, and abroad.

In 2008 and again in 2014, Drucker was recognized by the French state as an *Entreprise du Patrimoine Vivant* (EPV), a quality label created in 2005 to promote craft skills and manufacturing excellence. It shares this distinction with world-renowned French companies such as Baccarat crystal, Chevillotte billiard tables, Tolix chair manufacturers, and Pouenat ironwork art. Because, today more than ever, around the globe, the Drucker chair evokes a French savoir-faire, much like Haute Couture and fine wine, the "handmade," and the "bespoke." A refined and elegant world, timeless and endearing.

Bruno Dubois

A TASTE FOR CHALLENGES

h e's an entrepreneur from another era, but very much a businessman of his time, juggling professional adventures, skills and passions. Foremost, Bruno Dubois is a strategist with a big heart, sensitive to the companies that are above all human stories. Fascinated by challenges and failing businesses, this man of industry is especially attentive to and interested in those serendipitous encounters that lie dormant for some time, only to reappear years later as the obvious choice. This was the case with Drucker.

In 1992, when this motorcycle enthusiast—as a young man, he had participated in numerous rallies, including Paris-Dakar—had just resold a Czech engineering firm, he heard about a business very different from anything he had known before. Maugrion, a rattan furniture company in the town of Bayeux in Normandy, was for sale. Interested, he investigated further and discovered the existence of another rattan furniture manufacturer, Drucker, specializing in terrace chairs. It was in difficulty and also for sale. Maugrion escaped him, as did Drucker. Thirteen years passed. In 2005, by twist of fate, he learned at a dinner that Drucker was again in the doldrums. A new challenge, a new opportunity. Bruno Dubois bought the business, relying once again on his instincts. But not only his instincts, because he guessed the potential of this longstanding name in furnishings and could already see a promising international perspective. Ten years later, this intuition became a reality.

Bruno Dubois was born in Normandy to a good provincial middle-class family. He inherited his entrepreneurial spirit from his father, the founder of a refinery near Le Havre. After his secondary education and preparatory classes at the Lycée Pasteur in Neuilly-sur-Seine, Bruno Dubois studied at *École Centrale* in Lille to graduate in 1967 as an engineer specializing in fluid mechanics. "At the time, I hoped to have a career in aeronautics," he says. For lack of airplanes to design, he became passionate about all other types of industrial design. He turned

towards computing, in particular the computerization of production, which was a new science at that time. His first job was at Cegos, a conglomerate of consulting firms, then at Steria. Next, in the 1980s, he joined a group of friends defecting from the American firm McKinsey, at the origin of the ABC agency, where he added a new dimension to his industrial experience. Beginning in 1988, he branched out on his own into a variety of fields not limited to production. His experience ranged from pharmaceuticals for what would become the Sanofi group, to luxury with Leonard, not to mention food with Best Food and Danone, and of course engineering with Yamaha when he bought the Motobécane company, the manufacturer of Mobylette. Bruno Dubois would also handle foreign real estate promotions, construction, building and cigarette manufacturing. He worked for the Sud Ouest press group, led the transitional management at the heart of the Bolloré group in sub-Saharan Africa, and headed the distribution of a large perfume chain. "For the most part, the rules of success are the same in all economic and industrial sectors," he explains. "Mastering them is the fruit of long experience. This was, and is, the key to the resurrection of Drucker."

Although he was born by the sea, Bruno Dubois is an enthusiast of mountains and skiing, a devourer of newspapers and an avid reader, especially of the classics. With Drucker, he has immersed himself in the world of creation and color. And, when the time comes to part from this endearing firm, he hopes to reconnect with his first love, that of painting, which he practiced abundantly during his youth. In this way, he can continue his work and rediscover this innate passion for color.

He guessed the potential of this longstanding name in furnishings and could already see a promising international perspective. Ten years later, this intuition became a reality.

Previous pages:
facing the warehouses,
palette of various seat models,
caning and colors.

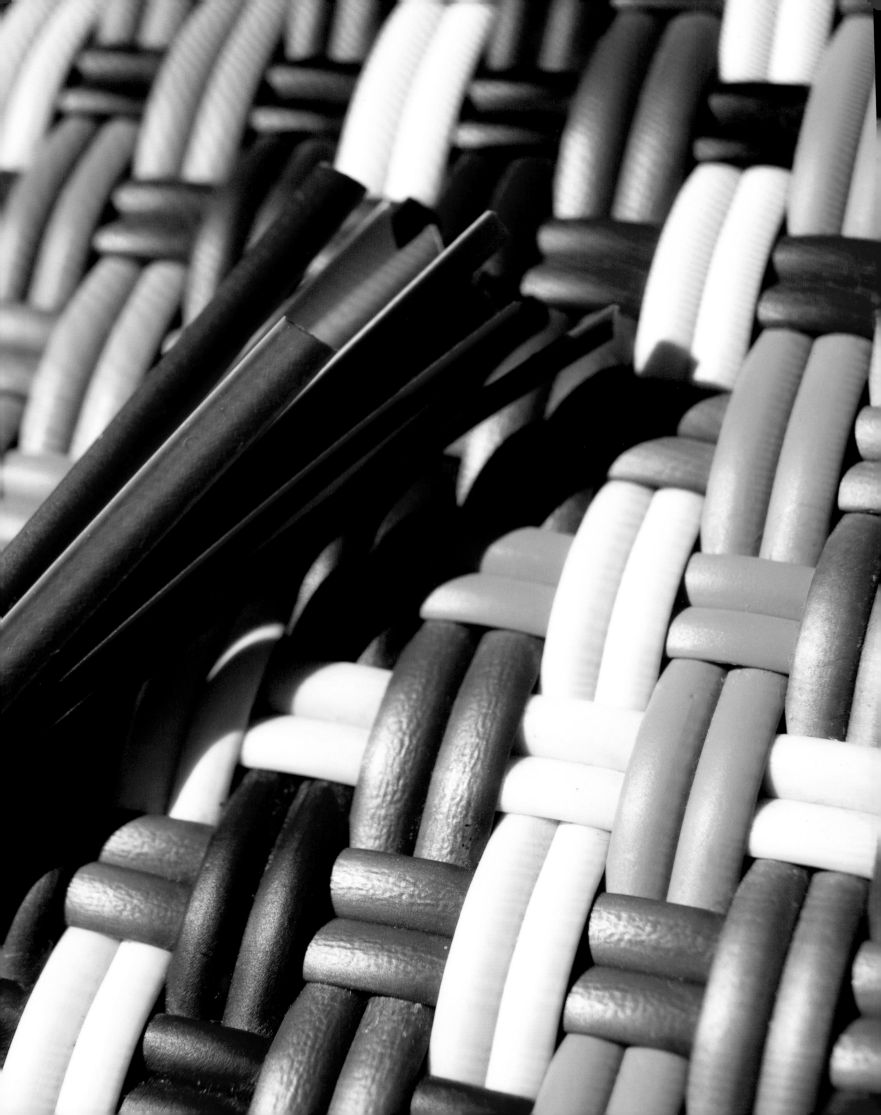

IN THE
Drucker
WORKSHOPS

At Drucker, every chair model is first projected onto paper, often inspired by a picture chosen from the company archives. *Manufacturing*, meanwhile, involves an ancestral savoir-faire, practiced in a workshop where life unfolds in near complete self-sufficiency. But this "monastic" life does not rule out the collaborations with the outside world that enrich the catalog each year with *contemporary new creations.* In this workshop, steeped in the *poetry of bygone crafts*, Drucker has been perpetuating for over a century the secrets of one of these artistic crafts that have earned France world-renowned reputation, without ever falling into nostalgia. Cutting, refining, grinding, steaming, bending, drying, weaving, assembling, and varnishing: these are the *stages in the manufacture* of a Drucker chair, followed by the choice of *colors*, which has become one of the creative highlights of the company. Because each chair here is the interpretation of an intelligent history of weaving and a passion for craftwork passed down through generations.

An Ancestral SAVOir-fAire

✕✕

in 1925, Drucker left Paris for Béthisy-Saint-Pierre, near Crépy-en-Valois, in the Oise department. A few decades later, in the 1970s, a fire forced the company to move a few kilometers away and establish its workshop in Gilocourt, in unoccupied buildings on the shores of the river Automne. Today, around thirty people work at the site, which includes both management and manufacturing. Some artisans carry out the actual weaving in their home. A career with Drucker starts early, and it usually lasts a lifetime, especially since the savoir-faire is traditionally handed down from generation to generation. Thus, assembly was once done by fathers and sons, while weaving was the responsibility of mothers and their daughters. Today, this division of labor between men and women continues, but recruitment is less and less within families.

The manufacture of seats is entirely artisanal. It involves a savoir-faire that is acquired over time, within the workshop. Five years of experience are needed to earn the title of "qualified fitter," and a few more years to justify a mastery of weaving.

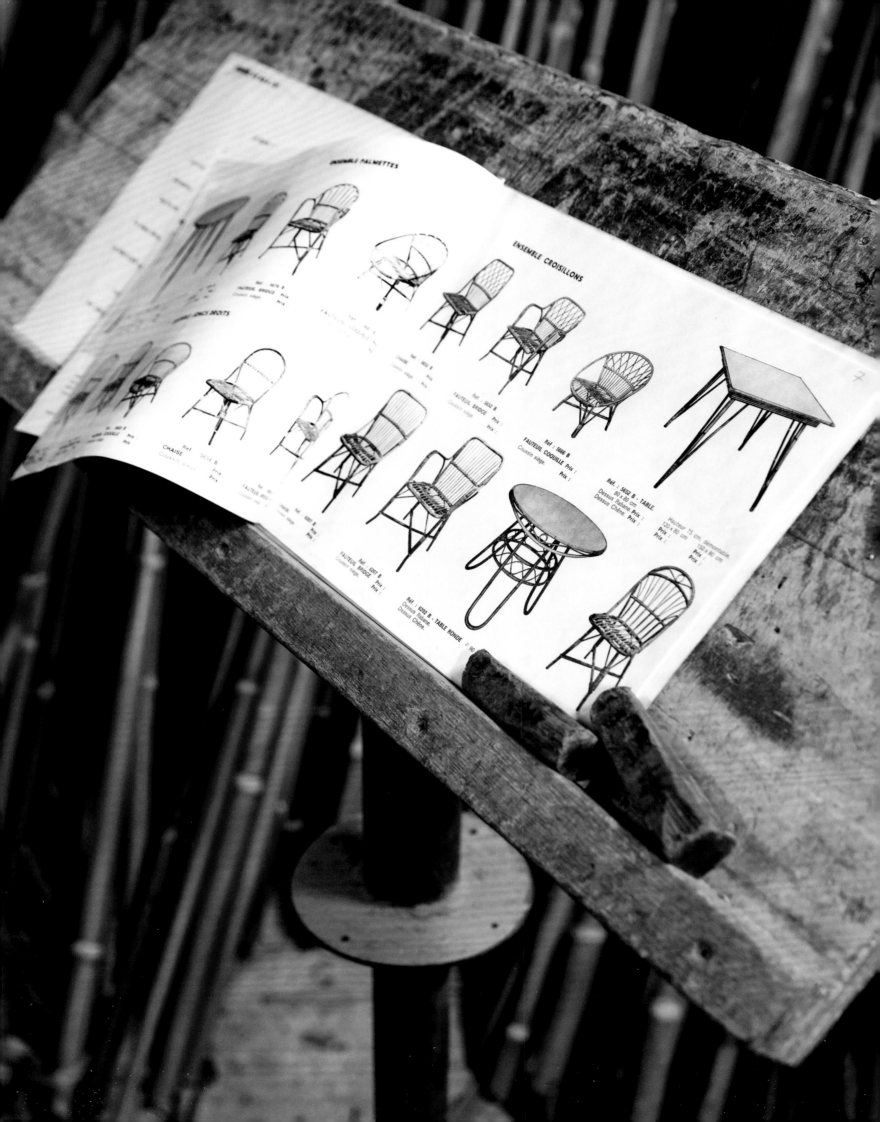

Manufacturing a Drucker chair therefore requires both great expertise and great dexterity. The craft also combines passion with a demand for excellence, just like artisanal arts such as the manufacture of crystal glass, porcelain, or fine leather. Not to mention that here, custom design covers everything down to the screws, nails and staples, most of which are specifically made for Drucker.

The making of a rattan chair, armchair, stool, flower box, high chair, bench, table or love seat, entirely by hand, demands at least six hours of work for the simplest model, and up to thirty hours for a sophisticated piece. The worthy artisans find it only natural that their most complicated pieces are described as "masterpieces," a name they have well earned.

The manufacture of seats is entirely artisanal. It involves a savoir-faire that is acquired over time, within the workshop.

Left page: beveled cut of Malacca cane; below, *Trèfle* armchair armrest torsion pattern.
Right page: a series of chair seats with classic diamond pattern caning with bicolor motif (black, white), being created in the workshops.

THE NINE STAGES OF THE CREATIVE PROCESS

Grown in Indonesia on the islands of Java and Sumatra, rattan is cut to lengths of three to five meters, then sorted by diameter and the frequency of nodes on the stem. Obviously, no two pieces are the same.

A corner of the Drucker workshop is reserved for the storage of rattan poles prior to cutting. Not far off are stacked wooden seating frames for chairs, armchairs and benches, of which there are twenty different models. New frames are regularly made to meet specific orders, when the necessary pieces have not yet been created for the stock. Most of the frames are built by Vosges carpenters, and those for benches, whether straight, curved or angled, are always made to measure. After the frames are delivered to the Drucker workshop, they are treated to strengthen them against all kinds of weather.

1) The first step to making rattan furniture consists of cutting the poles into segments to meet the structural needs of the seats, legs, backs and arms, based on their diameter and the location of the nodes. These sections are then refined and the nodes carefully sanded. This work requires great expertise.

Left page: molds for bending backs; pole straighteners, low stool, Victoria caning; torch "heater," prior to bending.

Right page: series of back frames
held by metal flanges.

2) Once prepared, the rattan segments are steamed
in a steam bath. The steamer at a hundred degrees
centigrade for twenty minutes provides the ideal
conditions to render the rattan suppler.

3) The next operation involves bending the rattan
using a mold to give it the correct form. There are
over a hundred molds, each corresponding to
a particular form, depending on whether one wishes
to obtain a bent or curved piece. Working with rattan
is much like working with clay, as the hand seeks to
define a figure, a volume, a design. And just like with
clay, time is not always on our side, since the plant
fiber, even damp, does not stay flexible for long.

Left page: anatomy of
a Drucker chair. Here diverse
elements of a *Marly* chair.
Basic stretched caning
(burgundy, gold, cream, black).

4) Once the piece is curved, it is left in its frame for three days so the sap liquefies during the steaming to crystallize, thereby ensuring that the rattan retains its designated shape. A repeated sanding then eliminates any last little imperfections.

5) The weaving stage, particularly demanding, requires concentration and experience. Indeed, each pattern corresponds to a different technique, the complex product of the intersection between warp and weft strips, somewhat equivalent to a jacquard weave for textiles.

To begin the seat, one must first staple strips to the wooden frame. Today, Drucker almost exclusively uses synthetic strips, either Rilsan or Raucord, boasting a wide color palette developed in-house. Natural strips, the only material available before the arrival of synthetic materials, are rarely selected, but may still be associated with Rilsan or Raucord. The former is obtained by slicing strips five millimeters wide and two millimeters thick from the rattan poles. In the past, this was then tinted or "glazed" as they used to say. However, it is now only used in its natural state since color has become the preserve of synthetic materials. Thus the weavers use

Rilsan, Raucord and, occasionally, natural strips. The most accomplished weavers, with at least ten years of experience, have a mastery of more than fifty different weave patterns. And though the seat may be flat, adapting the weaving to the sometimes complex forms of the chair backs increases the level of difficulty. This is why we talk about weaving the backs in three dimensions. No wonder the weaving workshop is so quiet.

6) Assembling the pre-curved parts, such as the legs, backs and arms of the armchairs, to create the frame is done using screws and nails made specifically for Drucker, perpetuating the assembly techniques of the nineteenth century. This work requires strength and skill, as well as experience, since there are many different models and their assembly can be tricky.

Previous pages: *Turenne* chair, Tartan caning (navy blue, gray, chocolate, white), back in the process of being woven to the left and finished to the right.

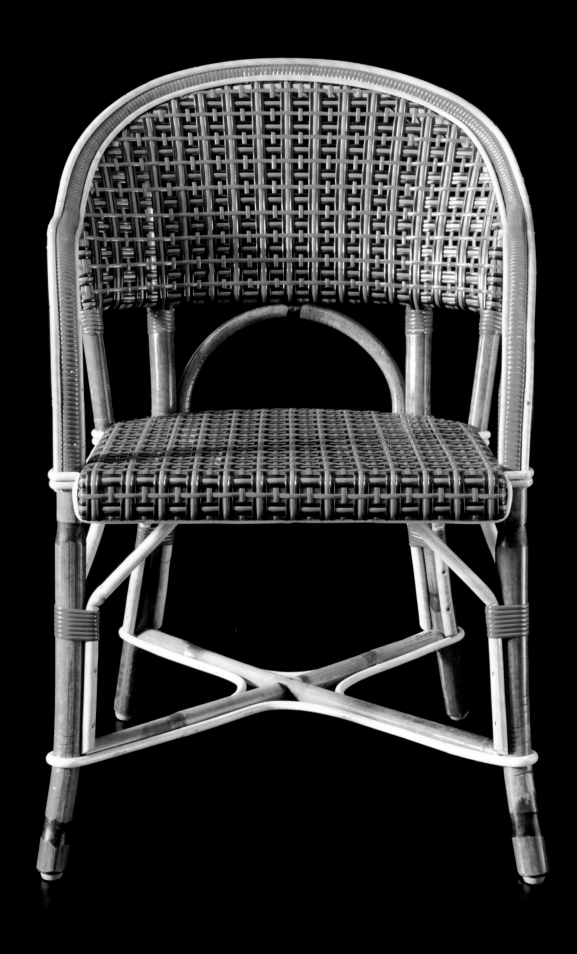

7) The weaving of backs and arms is performed on the assembled frame. After assembly, it is sent to the weaving workshop so that the back and arms receive their caning, usually the same as that of the seat, except when some decorators request a variation. This second phase of weaving is often more complex than that of the seat, firstly because the back and arms can be more sophisticated, and secondly because it goes without saying that the alignment of strips must always ensure continuity and regularity of the design to give the seat a harmonious line.

8) The wrapping, which involves concealing the stapling of the strips to the frame, is characteristic of the traditional aesthetics of rattan chairs. It is made with a double wrap of thin rattan split in two.

Previous pages, left page: *Haussmann* armchair, classic Fouquet's caning (tobacco, brown, brick); right page: base assemblage of the *Breban* chair. Left page: "balloons masterpieces" caning, created using a cobbler's instrument. Right page: back of a *Métier* armchair. Classic Odéon caning (tobacco, Gitane blue).

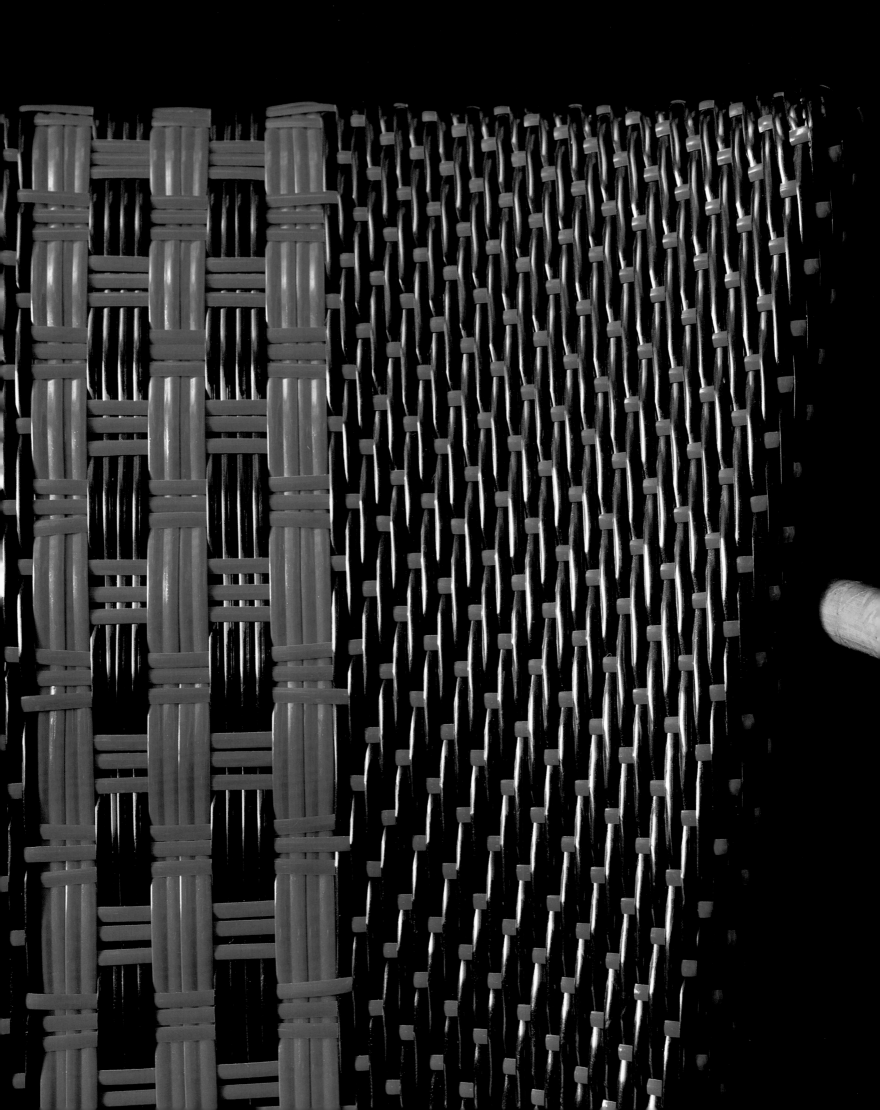

9) The finishes are first of all for a general control of quality. The legs are adjusted to ensure perfect stability and then they are shoed with protective "domes" at their base to give years of protection to furniture that is primarily intended for bistro terraces. Finally, they are varnished with products that are very resistant to ultraviolet rays and abrasive wear.

Previous double pages: Left, *Luxembourg* armchair "disheveled," before stapling and weaving of the bulged edging in white Rilsan; right, a trio of *Drouot* chairs, classic *Victoria* chairs (white, navy blue).

FROM NATURAL SHADE TO COLOR

Rattan cane had long been used in its natural state, with a preference for a slightly glazed appearance. In 1920 rattan began to take on colors, thanks to the tinting machines manufactured by the *Société Anonyme du Rotin*, which from then on offered a whole range of colors. Drucker was one of the first companies to have taken advantage of this new technique, quickly displaying an outstanding imaginative ability to offer many designs combining several colors. The current range, rich with models of weaving developed since then, is the legacy of a hundred years of inventiveness.

In the 1950s, the colored glazed rattan was replaced by Rilsan, which is resistant to sunlight, harsh weather and the passage of time. And available in thirty colors. Another synthetic fiber, Raucord, more recent but with comparable qualities, comes in sixteen colors, specifically designed for Maison Drucker. Unlike the very shiny Rilsan, Raucord is slightly satiny therefore highly popular with interior designers. For over seven years, the management of color ranges, the creation of unprecedented tones and their associations has been in the hands of colorist Amandine Gallienne, who oversees not only existing weaves, but also the creation of new ones.

In addition to manufacturing, Drucker also ensures the restoration of pieces sometimes over a century old. It repairs the ravages of time and refreshes seats put to the test day after day on café terraces. Artisans and weavers deploy their talents to thoroughly erase the damage of a long history, or to recreate an identical collection piece: just as others strive to restore luster to the gold braid of a frayed Genoa velvet, or replace a missing pearl on a tiara, or reinvigorate the faded paint on an old canvas. To this end, the Maison has carefully preserved the molds and jigs of all its models since its origins.

THE CRAFT OF THE RATTAN WORKER

The rattan techniques, although still taught at the *École Nationale d'Osiériculture et de Vannerie* in Fayl-Billot, Haute-Marne, are now those of an endangered profession. The rattan art and industry having often been associated with those of basketry, rattan workers were frequently recruited from among basket weavers, particularly during the interwar years, by the manufacturers Raguet, Petitot, Garnier and Drucker. When the learning was not done in school, it was usually acquired in the company with an apprenticeship generally lasting two years. In practice, this apprenticeship is much longer today, requiring many years of observation and workshop practice.

In the eighteenth century, rattan work involved a whole series of operations. They included splitting the canes, separating the splices, twisting, weaving and caning the rattan fiber, completing the seat, the chair back or table top, and finally lacquering the finished structure. All of these tasks were accomplished under the careful guidance of their respective expert craftsmen. These techniques are now no longer implemented, except perhaps at the corner of a fair or exhibition, to show off a rather spectacular savoir-faire that is now purely picturesque.

Low stools with round cushion. Classic checkerboard caning (black, white, aluminum).

TOOLS OF THE PAST

The tools required to create a rattan chair, armchair or other piece of furniture reflect a beautiful constancy since the eighteenth century. Certainly the technical innovations of the industrial era have entered manufacturing, such as cast iron boilers and, in the twentieth century, galvanized steel tubs. But the French names of some tools used by the rattan worker still carry with them the charm of forgotten crafts.

VOCABULARY

ARLEQUIN: a tool used for bending a rattan rod preheated to a hundred degrees. After blocking part of the rod in the arlequin, it is bent by weighing heavily on the handle of the latter.

BATTE: an iron tool with a ring and a handle to straighten canes after they have been steamed and become malleable. The baton is passed into the ring, and by putting pressure on the handle, the desired deformation is achieved.

ÉPLUCHOIR OR ÉMONDOIR: a cutting tool for pruning, or removing what is unnecessary from the rattan rod.

FENDOIR: a tool used for splitting rattan canes in two.

PLANAGE: the act of beveling one piece of rattan in order to join it with another.

PLANE: a concave bladed tool with two handles, for planage operations.

*To pack up the terraces,
the lightweight
and sturdy chairs
are stacked for storage
or for transportation
on the back.*

Left page: piled in the store,
Chenonceau chairs with Victoria
caning in Raucord (black,
chocolate, white).
Right page: above, a trio of
Drapeau chairs: France striped
caning (Gitane blue, white, red)
Sweden, bicolor caning (Gitane
blue, yellow) and Italy striped
caning (pine green, white, red).
Below, panel of *Chenonceau*
chairs in Raucord herringbone
(olive green, light green) and
checkerboard caning in Raucord
(white, black, ivory, beige) and
France chairs, striped caning
(Gitane blue, white, red).

Set of
ColoRs

Right page: glossy brilliance, the rolls of Rilsan in colors that yell!

Amandine Gallienne

a fter attending the *École Nationale Supérieure d'Arts de Paris-Cergy* (Ensapc) and a school of graphic arts, Amandine Gallienne started out as a designer at Euro RSCG Design, where she was responsible for visual identity, graphic design and signage. She followed in the footsteps of her mother, well-known in advertising for her work at the Carré Noir agency, and her father who made his career at UGC. Her parents had also successfully relaunched a Bordeaux vineyard inherited from a grandparent, Château Faugères, which they would separate from thereafter. Having inherited that same taste for change and challenges, the young woman left Euro RSCG Design to go out on her own and pursue a number of freelance projects, including the signage for Hôpital Saint-Joseph-Saint-Luc in Lyon. In this way, she laid the foundation for what would be her new life, that of a self-taught colorist. Because color is something she has always had within her, ever since she was a child, thanks to her paternal grandmother, "an original, modern woman who loved bright and contrasting colors," she says, and who took her on walks through the galleries and museums of Paris. Still today, it is in the flamboyant tones of modern and abstract painting that the young woman stimulates her own palette. 2004 brought a new direction. She took off on a world tour, just to discover the colors of elsewhere, those of fashion, decoration, the ones that adorn the architecture of the many countries she visited. From her travels, she returned with large notebooks filled with chromatic variations gleaned from the dyers, colorists and painters she met.

"The idea was simple," she says. "Bring together a collection of colors of the world." And since Amandine Gallienne loves to share the things she likes, she presented four hundred photographs that year from her trip in the exhibition *Collection de Couleurs*, at the Galerie des Galeries Lafayette. The following year she published *Un monde de couleurs* with Thames & Hudson to leave a visual and written testimony of her journey which was much more than an initiation.

Charmed by this world of hers, Bruno Dubois asked her to become the colorist of Drucker, especially as color was becoming a trump card to convey the image of the company abroad. Since 2008, the young woman has dedicated her passion and talent to this creator of rattan furniture that evokes, in her view, a unique triptych: "excellence, freedom and joy." Giving rhythm to the sharp and pastel tones in weaves of chairs, armchairs, tables and stools, Amandine Gallienne measures out no more than four different tones, and plays on contrasts, gloss and matte effects. She works more and more with rattan and Rilsan colors as she would with textile fibers.

At Drucker, Amandine Gallienne rules the world of color with the grace of a queen. Here, color arises from associations of materials, and therefore from the weaving. Her laboratory is her home, a place with walls in yellow and blue, green and violet. However her atelier is neutral gray in order not to affect the color ranges being constructed. Her inspirational books are the big notebooks in which she writes preferably in blue or indigo ink, her tone of choice, even if red is still her favorite color. Red is found teamed with pink in the *Titanic* chair, a bestseller in a fairly simple cane: "Red is the color *par excellence*," she says, "It is the most striking, the most flamboyant, the most passionate, the most absolute. This is the original color, the most beautiful of colors. Indigo rather reminds me of a material, an odor, particular chromatic variations. It is also quite a fascinating tone from a societal point of view. In Asia for example, the indigo plant is grown on balconies or in gardens to dye fabrics."

Her inspirations? Architecture, street fashion, fashion in general, a forest walk, a light, a painting and contemporary art, which she will reinterpret without following the trends of the moment: "If there are modes in terms of color, their symbolism, however, does not change every year," she says. "At Drucker, it is true that manufacturing constraints influence the design, and it would be illusory to believe that one creates new color ranges for each season. My work consists rather in orchestrating different combinations and harmoniously composing between colors and weaves, to bring life to new combinations from the existing color palette of thirty-two basic colors."

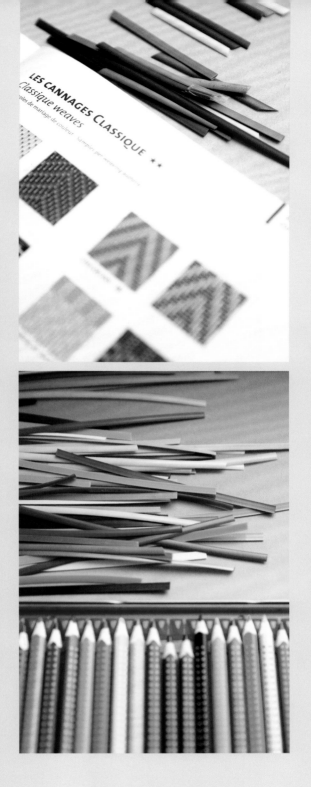

Attentive to Mone and Bruno Dubois's comments and suggestions, Amandine Gallienne prepares samples and proposes a set of different ranges twice a year. Following the manufacturing with an outsider's eye, she occasionally allows herself to change a small detail in the design of a chair, with the agreement of the company, as in the case of the *Confidence* chair.

Always ready to rise to a challenge, Amandine Gallienne has been engaged in such diverse work as the definition of the style guide for the Fondation Chirac, the signage of the *Maison et Objet* home show, the color of the wall of a public housing building in Chevilly-Larue, the chromatic palette of the season for "lifestyle" products at Hermès, the color of the illustrations for the album *Le Loup est un loup pour l'homme* by Philippe Katerine and Julien Baer (2014). She also works for the "Petit h" line of objects, led by Pascale Mussard at Hermès, as well as for the Swiss hosiery house Molli. Wishing to share her passion, she has been teaching since 2012 at the *Écoles d'Art Américaines* in Fontainebleau—famous for linking architecture and music—and is involved in the Atelier de Sèvres, a prep school for competitive entrance exams to major art schools. "I try to teach them that color is a material rather than a simple decoration," she concludes. "It is a tool of construction and design to emphasize a shape, enhance an element, or tell a story."

She enhances tones, develops patterns, tries bold and one-of-a-kind combinations; her taste is as valuable as every trend. Her unique perspective pushes the boundaries when the material synthesizes color.).

RILSAN AND RAUCORD:
SYNTHETIC WEAVING MATERIALS...
QUITE NATURALLY

Today, in an environment that encourages the development of ecological philosophies and despite the importance given to preserving biodiversity, split rattan is still being replaced by PVC (polyvinyl chloride), polyethylene and, especially, Rilsan strips. This natural polyamide material derived from castor oil is perfectly suited to weaving for outdoor furniture. Manufactured by Arkema, Rilsan has been used by Drucker for many years due to its many positive qualities including longevity; flexibility, even after many years of use and exposure to temperatures ranging from -50°C to +70°C; resistance to insects, fungi, mold and termites; fastness of its colors and brilliance, able to withstand UV rays, rain, snow, and salt. Finally, Rilsan is distinguished by its ease of maintenance, since it can be cleaned simply with soap and water.

Raucord, a high-density polyethylene produced by the German firm Rehau, specializing in engineering plastics, has qualities quite comparable to those of Rilsan. With its satin almost matte texture, it is particularly praised by some interior designers put off by the high gloss of Rilsan.

Rilsan or Raucord? The choice is based on purely aesthetic criteria: the brilliance of the first, the velvetiness of the second.

Left page: Rilsan, brilliant finish, existing in 30 colors.
Right page: Raucord, satin finish, existing in 16 colors.

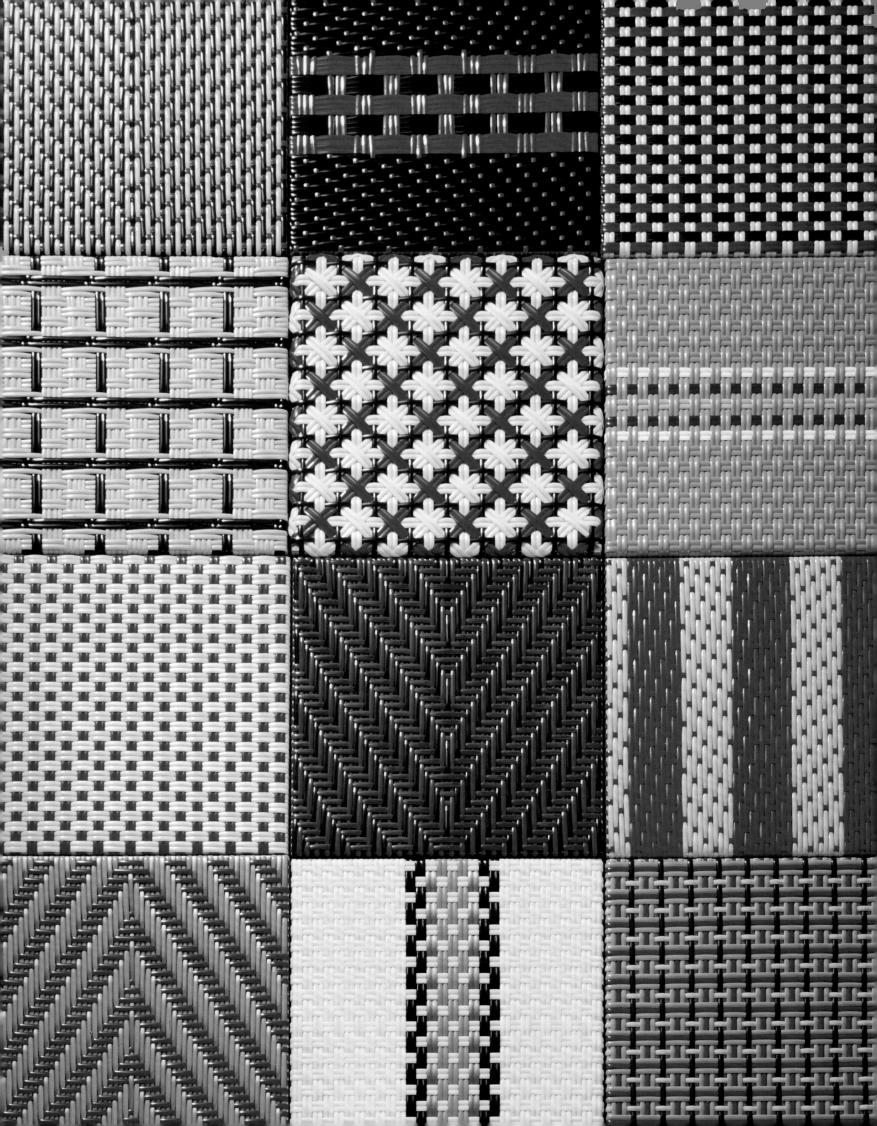

DRUCKER
PARIS

depuis 1885

COLORIS **RILSAN** ® DISPONIBLES / **RILSAN** ® AVAILABLE COLORS

Vert Sapin / Pine Green	Bleu Marine / Marine Blue
Vert Nil / Nile Green	Bleu Gitane / Gipsy Blue
Vert Jade / Jade Green	Bleu Pétrole / Petroil Blue
Vert Menthe / Mint Green	Bleu Azur / Sky Blue
Bordeaux / Burgundy	Vert d'Eau / Water Green
Brique / Brick	Tabac / Tabacco
Rouge / Red	Chocolat / Chocolate
Rose / Pink	Marron / Brown
Vieux Rose / Old Rose	Havane / Havane
Noir / Black	Mastic / Mastic
Alu / Aluminium	Mandarine / Mandarin
Gris / Grey	Crème / Cream
Blanc / White	Jaune / Yellow
Fuschia / Fushia	Ivoire / Ivory
Parme / Violet	Or / Gold
Glycine / Wisteria	

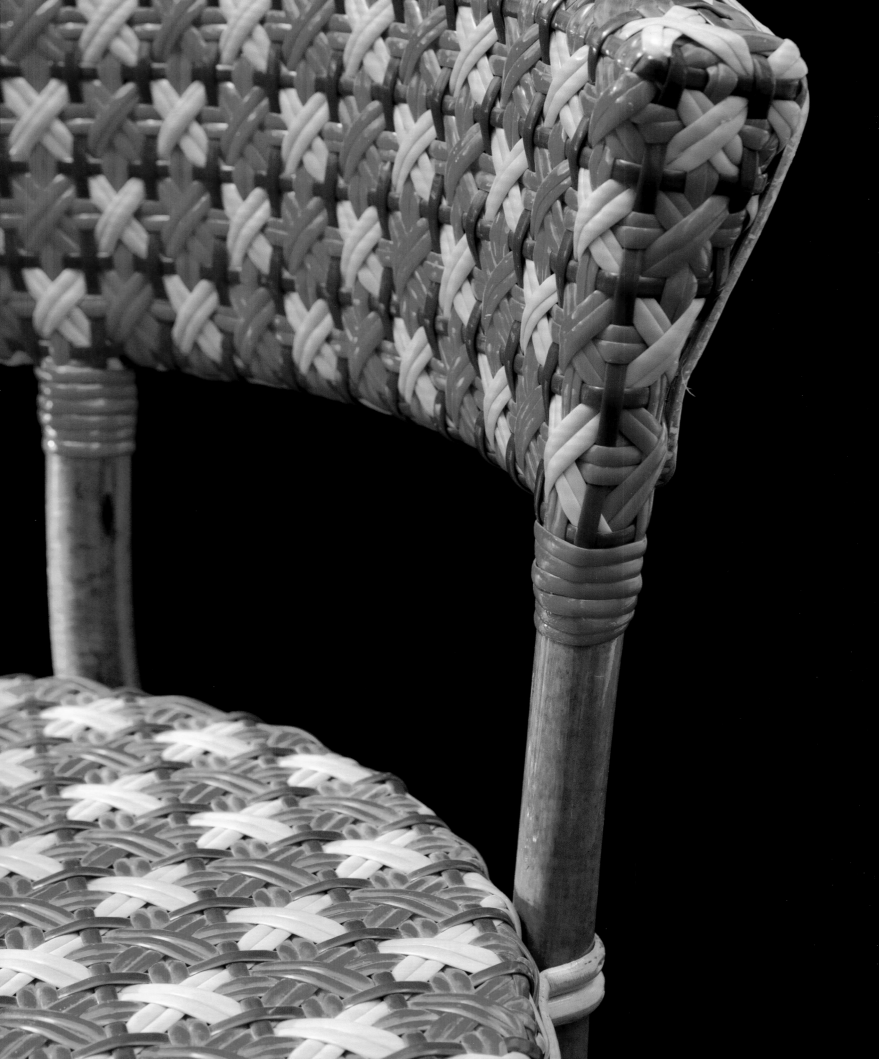

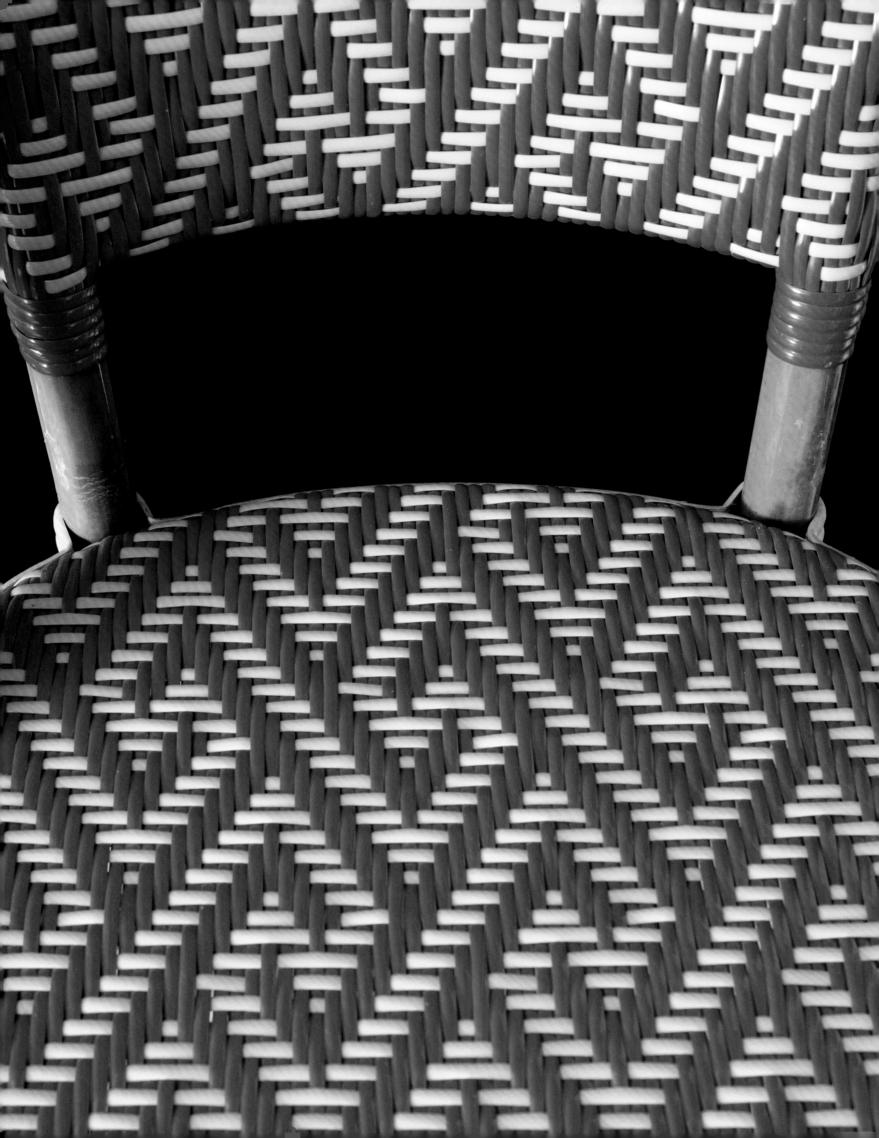

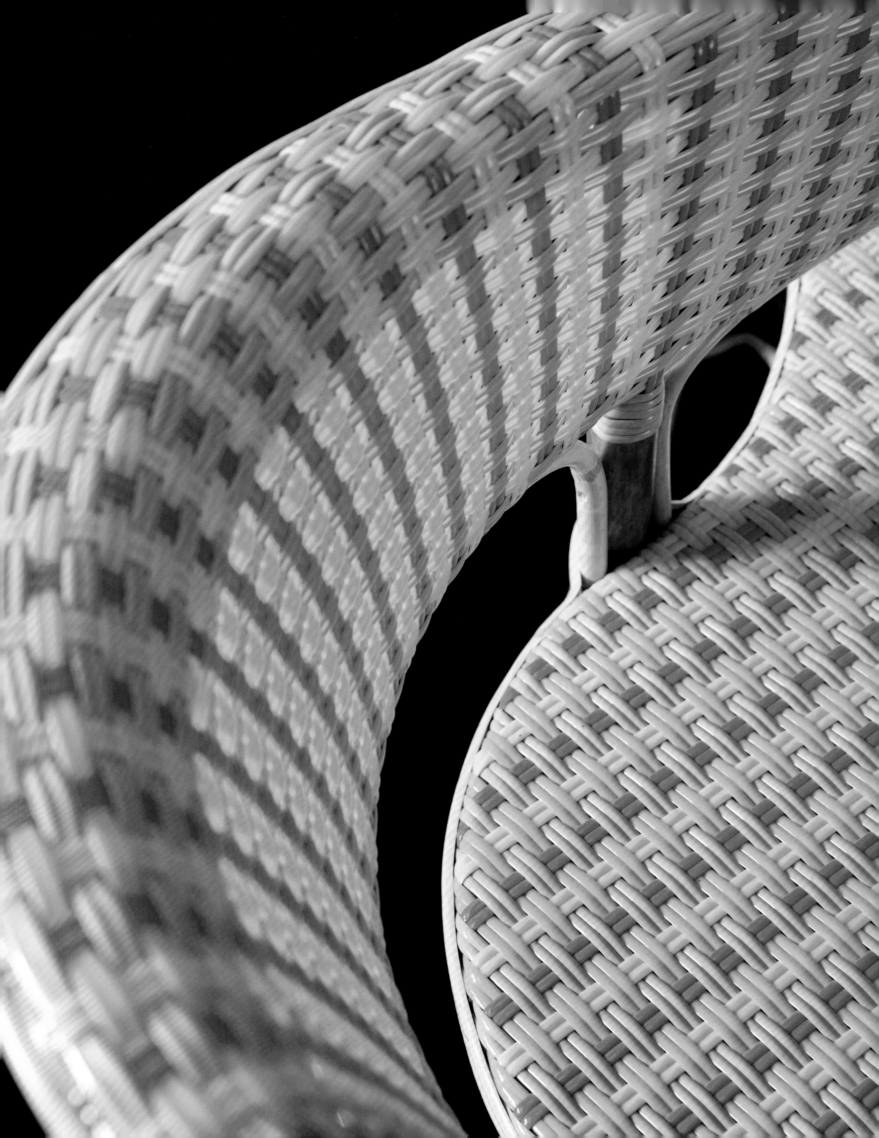

The seat
in all its forms

VARIATIONS

on the Drucker Chair

Architects and interior designers around the world have not only used rattan furniture to bring their projects to life, but also wished to design Drucker collection models themselves. Some have simply used existing designs, such as *Jacques Grange*, while changing the shapes, sizes, weaves and color combinations. Others have reinterpreted the story of a legendary brand in their own way without dominating it, thus showing its creative richness and ability to adapt to the world of today while retaining its poetry and its identity. But the majority of designers have rather played with existing weaves and colors to give their personal touch. Adding to the existing collections, their creations have thus become genuine sources of inspiration. This was the case with *Christian Biecher*, *Patrick Norguet*, *India Mahdavi* and *François Champsaur*, who completely redesigned one of the company's flagship seats to make it a bestseller.

As Bruno Dubois explains, "Most of the designers we have teamed with were familiar with the brand before working with it. This was the case with Philippe Starck, someone Maurice Drucker would have liked to entrust with the future of his company before selling it. He had already guessed that the image and development of Drucker would advance through design."

After buying the company, Bruno Dubois expanded its offering by inviting the great talents of the day to work on it, and by participating in interior design exhibitions like *Maison et Objet* to reveal and showcase the incredible color palette of its creations. The media coverage that followed and the work with major French, English and American interior design agencies helped develop a décor library with thousands of photographs. The result of this more international focus is the export of 60% of production.

The *Cardinal* Armchair,
by FRANÇOIS **CHAMPSAUR**

A graduate of the *École Supérieure des Beaux-Arts* in Marseille and the *École Nationale Supérieure des Arts Décoratifs* in Paris, François Champsaur founded his agency in 1996. His early creations revolved around the emblematic places of the capital and the provinces, such as the Café de l'Alma in Paris, or the Maison Troisgros in Roanne. His success quickly led to other equally renowned projects. His interventions at Hôtel Le Metropolitan, Hôtel du Ministère and Hôtel Vernet in Paris, Hôtel Royal in Évian, and Le Poulpe restaurant in Marseille, not to mention many private apartments, are all powerful and original achievements expressing his guiding philosophy: "to make understated interiors that are not places of representation." Attracted to artistic crafts, since 1996 he has also been designing furniture and fixtures in oak, birch, Tavel or Burgundy stone, wrought iron, steel and lacquered metal. Notably, he launched the HC28 furniture collection for the Asian market. Collaborations ensued with First Time, Treca Interiors, Toulemonde Bochart carpets and, more recently, with the ironwork company Pouenat and Ravel pottery. He thus remains faithful to what he has always loved: nature, light, simple materials, authentic houses, and clean lines that radiate a beautiful serenity.

François Champsaur had already worked with Maison Drucker fifteen years ago to design a stackable rattan chair for Café de l'Alma in Paris. Since then, the passion that the architect designer feels for the company has not wavered. "I have always loved the savoir-faire of the company, and particularly the ambiguity of this rattan material, which cultivates a character both traditional and contemporary. Especially since it is a complicated

fiber to work with. However, as soon as we accept its suppleness and constraints, the exercise becomes particularly creative." For the *Cardinal* armchair, the specifications were simple. The aim was to create a comfortable rattan armchair, in different sizes, and especially without the slightest use of plastic. "The challenge was to create a shape from a single vine," he explains. Originally, this chair was designed to equip Le Poulpe restaurant in Marseille, which eventually changed its mind. But its shape and color were sufficiently original that Maison Drucker did not want to leave this research as a sketch, so it was added to its collections. Its baptismal name was also changed. It had almost been called "Poulpe," French for "octopus," not only because of the restaurant for which it had been intended, but especially because of the single vine worked like a tentacle. Finally, it was its red color that carried the day and determined its name.

François Champsaur concludes, "Drucker is the perfect example of a company in keeping with its history and its time. It is a company that has remained open to contemporary creation and to the future. It knew how to resist the tidal wave of globalization and cheap consumer goods that led to the disappearance of so many crafts. Fortunately, today, a number of French companies are still there to bear witness to this living heritage that is craftsmanship. So, it has been a pleasure to work with artisans who are passionately in love with their craft, and who are eager to preserve their savoir-faire, while remaining curious and attentive to what comes along."

The *Chippendale* Chair and Stool,
by GILLES & BOISSIER

Together in life and in work, Dorothée Boissier and Patrick Gilles infuse everything they handle with a special magic touch. After their respective studies at *École Supérieure d'Arts Graphiques Penninghen* and *École Camondo*, they began their career at Christian Liaigre. This is where they met. They founded their own agency in 2004 and achieved many private and public projects worldwide. Recently, a mega-yacht of 55 meters, the *Atlante*, and hotels (the Four Seasons in Mexico City, the Mandarin Oriental in Marrakech, the first Baccarat Hotel in New York) show that they are equally at home with gargantuan projects as with renovations that are more discreet, playful and "intellectual," such as the Chess Hotel in Paris in 2015. With their own identifiable touch, they have also revamped restaurants (Hakkasan in Dubai, Abu Dhabi and Las Vegas, Buddakan in New York, Kinugawa, Tong Yen and the Hexagone in Paris) and stores (Revillon, Moncler, Baccarat in Paris, Hogan in Munich). This powerhouse décor couple also participate in diverse exhibitions, such as *AD Intérieurs* in 2013 and 2014, *Oxymores #01 and #02* in 2014, where they presented—amongst a collection of art photography by John Stewart, Melvin Sokolsky and Albert Watson—their first collection of custom-made furniture: *Gilles & Boissier Privé*. Dorothée Boissier and Patrick Gilles both adore arts and crafts, the essence of rare woods, clean and fluid lines, volumes with soul, and soft, enveloping colors. Like no other, they handle the spectacular and the intimate, the rigorous and the jovial. In short, everything that stirs emotion.

Dorothée Boissier explains, "Working with Maison Drucker was an obvious choice. Their creations have stood for more than a century on all the terraces of Paris, and their expertise is universally recognized. So it only seemed normal for us to invite them to make a custom model we were planning for the terrace of a Miami restaurant." When the couple contacted the company, it was in fact for a specific project, a matching chair and stool for Makoto, a Japanese restaurant in Miami. And though this first creation displayed Japanese influences in keeping with the spirit of the place, it was then reproduced in a different finish for La Villa restaurant in Paris. The designers met with Bruno Dubois, who talked with them about his business with such passion it was infectious. Dorothée Boissier continues, "We were impressed by the number of chair designs in the archives that had never been reissued, and we were captivated by the shapes of these very romantic 1900s models that looked as if like they had been made solely of entwined rattan vines. And since Drucker savoir-faire is incomparable, the final result of our stool and chair was obviously perfect."

The *Tuileries* Chair,
by INDIA **MAHDAVI**

/

A graduate in architecture from the *École Nationale Supérieure des Beaux-Arts* in Paris, in industrial design from Cooper Union in New York, and in graphic design and furniture from Parsons School of Design in New York, India Mahdavi began her career in the 1990s at Christian Liaigre where she went on to become artistic director. From this experience in the school of rigor and monochrome, she has forged a style all of her own that is glamorous, sensual and colorful. In 1999, she founded her design studio on Rue Las Cases in Paris, inaugurated her first showroom next door four years later, and then launched her first furniture line. In 2012, she opened a second boutique of small objects, and, in parallel, decorated private homes and public places famous worldwide, such as the APT lounge bar in New York, the hotels Condesa df in Mexico and L'Apogée in Courchevel, the Gallery gastro-brasserie at Sketch in London, the Germain restaurants in Paris and I love Paris by Guy Martin at Charles de Gaulle airport. She has also designed a collection of cement tiles for Bisazza, carpets for La Manufacture Cogolin, and *Parrot* tables for Petite Friture. Countless creations on which she leaves a watermark of her Iranian-Egyptian origins and poetically mixes with Western decorative trends.

The encounter between India Mahdavi and Maison Drucker occurred when the Beaumarly group, led by Gilbert and Thierry Costes, creators of the finest cafés and restaurants of Paris, entrusted her with the renovation of Café Français, Place de la Bastille. She says, "Maison Drucker is part of our identity. These armchairs and chairs are the reason we recognize the terrace of a French café." The first *Tuileries* model that the architect designer created for Drucker is the *Candy Chair* "whose colors are reminiscent of bonbons, or sugary little amuse-bouches," she describes.
The next creation, the *Vichy Chair* is a variation thereof. These two folding chairs are also included in the "petits objets" collection in her Paris boutique. "For these two models, I worked the motif as if it were a textile. The chairs have appeared in many interior design projects."
India Mahdavi concludes, "Our adventure with Drucker is far from over. We continue to work together on residential and public projects."

/

The *Rive Gauche* Chair, by Andrée Putman,
Presented by OLIVIA **PUTMAN**

After graduating with a degree in art history from the *Sorbonne*, Olivia Putman first set sail in the world of contemporary painting. She then changed direction in the 1990s by creating the association Usines Ephémères, with the objective of reviving disused premises. Her next passion was for land art, becoming a landscape architect and working for two years with Louis Benech, namely on the redevelopment of the Jardins des Tuileries in Paris. She pursued this activity solo when she created, among other projects, the gardens and terraces of the Pagoda House in Tel Aviv. In 2007, she became artistic director of Studio Putman and began her career in the legendary agency by renovating the Morgans Hotel in New York, reimagined by her mother. She then designed a line of outdoor furniture for Fermob, a collection of eyeglass frames, carpets for Toulemonde Bochart, and furniture for Silvera. She organized the scenography of the Madeleine Vionnet exhibition at the Musée des Arts Décoratifs in Paris, created a fabric collection for Pierre Frey in 2011, and then assumed the artistic direction of the Lalique company. So many realms in which she expresses her concept of luxury, which lies more in the justness of things than in their shine. "Drucker, first of all, is a dazzle of colors, like in a Jacques Demy film;" she says. "As a little girl, I had already fallen under the spell of the combination of rough and raw rattan and brilliant plastic weave. Later I felt the desire to understand the savoir-faire of this company that really deserves to be valued and protected. If only to defend the values it embodies, its art, its identity, its obsession with quality, and its respect for creation."

Before joining Studio Putman in 2007, Olivia Putman, then a landscape architect, often went to the manufacturer in Gilocourt to select chairs that would brighten the gardens of clients who had entrusted her with their property. "Paris, bistros and cafés come immediately to my mind when I think of Drucker chairs," she continues. "Their reassuring forms belong to our collective memory. Each creation is a kind of link between yesterday and today. I have had one for over ten years, and even today it is like new." For this project, the designer focused primarily on optimizing production costs, so that her creation could be proposed at an affordable price. "I like to design objects for daily use, and that can blend into any kind of atmosphere. I imagine this chair just as well on a terrace overlooking the Alpilles as in a very contemporary kitchen. This is, incidentally, what I want when I design an object. I want it to be likeable, that is to say, worthy of love, so that it best accompanies our daily life, or even that it embellishes it." If Olivia Putman baptized her chair *Rive Droite*, it was not only as a tribute to Paris, but also to evoke a change in lifestyle or direction. "My family was very Rive Gauche, and *Rive Gauche* was the name my mother Andrée Putman had given the chair she designed for Drucker. I only really discovered the Rive Droite a few years ago, and since then I have completely adopted it."

The *Saint-Michel* Armchair, by JACQUES **GRANGE**

He decorates the most famous apartments and houses around the world, as well as hotels, restaurants, and the showrooms of prestigious brands. He is currently working on the image of the new Marc Jacobs store, and for the Olsen sisters' label in New York. He is creating a hotel in Lyon with Jean-Michel Wilmotte and has designed the scenography for the exhibition of the Yves Saint Laurent and Jacques Doucet collections. Jacques Grange is at the origin of this French and elegant art of living that has been widely copied. He cultivates cross-creation, mixing furniture of great value and charming objects that express the melody of feelings, masterly paintings and simple collages.

The interior designer discovered Maison Drucker in cafés, at Café de Flore in Saint-Germain-des-Prés in Paris, among others, "simply by looking at what I was sitting on," he reveals. But he already knew the company well and had used its creations in many previous projects, in particular for the Cinecittà café in Francis Ford Coppola's hotel Palazzo Margherita, in Bernalda, Italy.

The company therefore naturally entrusted him with the reinterpretation of one of its classics, the *Saint-Michel* armchair, for the Cappuccino café in Madrid. It was not a question of form, as the model already existed, but rather creating a new range of colors. "This first collaboration was the result of serendipity," confides Jacques Grange. "Drucker is a mix of tradition, charm and quality: a timeless universe diffusing an eternal fragrance, transmitted from generation to generation. That said, I've always loved rattan furniture: the pieces of the Second Empire, the ones we saw with Jean Cocteau or at Madeleine Castaing's. They contain something that is both fragile and strong, poetic and nostalgic."

The *Royal* Armchair,
by Christian **Biecher**

Architect, designer and urban planner, Christian Biecher has designed and led many private and public projects in France and Europe or Asia: the Tur buildings in Tokyo and Harvey Nichols department store in Hong Kong in 2004, the renovation of the Budapest Stock Exchange in 2011, then a set of office buildings in Prague and the new Le Printemps store in Strasbourg, as well as major urban projects such as the Bois-Sauvage neighborhood in Évry and modernization of La Grande-Motte. This virtuoso of clean lines and spaces bathed in light graduated in 1989 from the *École Nationale Supérieure d'Architecture* in Paris-Belleville. He also excels in the design of decorative objects for prestigious international brands, including Baccarat, Christofle, Lancôme, and Manufacture Nationale de Sèvres, and for galleries like Néotù, a precursor of modern movements, or Cat-Berro. From the start, the achievements of Christian Biecher have made the headlines, with the renovation of the Korova restaurant in Paris to the *Trois-Roses* vase designed for Baccarat in 1998. His success is such that he had a personal exhibition devoted to him at the Musée des Arts Décoratifs in Paris in 2002, and his work is included in the collections of the Design Museum in Lisbon and the Centre National d'Art et de Culture Georges Pompidou in Paris. After having defined and created the concept for Fauchon establishments in Tokyo and Beijing in 2006 and 2007, Christian Biecher was entrusted in 2008 with the renovation of Café Fauchon on Place de La Madeleine in Paris, followed by the development of sites for Fauchon in Dubai and Casablanca in 2009 and 2010. For this flagship of excellence in French gastronomy, silver and pink tones were favored. The furniture was ordered from Drucker, including this armchair whose metal frame dressed in elegant Rilsan challenges the rattan specialist's traditional codes of style. It is the ideal match: two internationally renowned Parisian names that work in perfect harmony.

The *Republica* Armchair,
by PATRICK NORGUET

Industrial designer Patrick Norguet is particularly fond of objects and the materials they are made of, in all their diversity, but he especially loves the places where they are born, namely factories and art workshops. This explains his taste for no-frill functional creations inspired by Scandinavian schools and Austrian schools alike. Fascinated by the history of objects, he has been devoted for over ten years to designing flagship creations for global brands (Arflex, Tacchini and Artifort, among others) on the international design scene.

Republica is the name that Patrick Norguet gave to his chair: a nod to the famous Place de la République in Paris, not far from where he established his agency. It was by chance that the designer discovered Maison Drucker, during a visit to the 2008 Equip'Hotel exhibition. Bruno Dubois had recently bought the company. "The history of this company immediately grabbed me," remembers Patrick Norguet. "It was a thunderbolt. The legacy of the past, the context, the production of this period, this very special tradition Drucker has forged with rattan. Everything was there to consider a collaboration."

The designer then contacted the company and proposed to work on developing new products in order to "write a sequel to the stories that already existed." As with all of his projects, he analyzed the company's profile before proposing to reinterpret a classic chair. By modernizing it, the chair could be produced industrially, ensuring its production on a larger scale.

"The world has changed," he says. "Part of the production has been relocated and usages have evolved."

A few months later, his preliminary research resulted in a creation combining synthetic Raucord weave and an aluminum frame. This was a first.

"It was a question of making an object that would be self-evident, designing a chair that would find its place in the collections of Maison Drucker, with a simple design and easy to understand. I wanted to give a contemporary dimension to a classic that would then be used in a variety of places, and this in a wide choice of finishes and uses."

Republica is therefore the fruit of a genuine reflection in design and its lines follow the logic of a singular product.

"For me, Maison Drucker represents an important period in the history of design. It evokes the ancient trade in raw materials between Asia and France, travel, the 1920s and the rise of bistro chairs. It illustrates an emblematic way of producing rattan from the nineteenth century until the First World War, and that subtle blend of craftsmanship and industrial production. I work for big brands of furniture, but my experience with this French family business has proved different and extremely rewarding."

A PROMENADE

around the Drucker Chair

We see it on the terraces of the most beautiful brasseries, cafés, restaurants and hotels of Paris, France and the whole world, often in spectacular locations.

In Paris, for the Café Français, the interior designer India Mahdavi specially designed a resolutely contemporary chair and produced it in a palette of red, white and blue. With its cane work in a checkerboard pattern of red and white that echoes the gingham tablecloths placed on tables, the *Parnasse* model brings poetry to the terrace of the Café Rey, also located on the edge of Place de la Bastille. There is greater diversity, however, on the Patio of the Hôtel Prince de Galles, with eight chairs of colorful cane work designed by Bruno Borrione, the interior designer who has been working with the agency of Philippe Starck since 1985 and co-founded the Starck + Borrione agency (S++B) in 2014.

This colorful tour continues by the sea in Étretat, at the Restaurant du Perrey, at La Salamandre, as well as at Hôtel Le Rayon Vert, on the beach, where the *Arc-en-ciel* chairs preside. It is not uncommon for the frames, weaving and colors to be designed to fit into a unique environment or décor, inspired by the story of a brasserie, or of its magic, like a jewel that enhances an outfit. Each institution has its chair, and each chair has its atmosphere. For example, the *Seine* model was made especially for Les Vapeurs restaurant in Trouville, an institution that cultivates nostalgia and Art Déco elegance, even in its style guide and its menus created by the poster designer Raymond Savignac. On the beach of Deauville, chairs of the famous Planches also distill the memory of the *Belle Époque* along with the seaside and summer atmosphere emanating from the town, not to mention the annual tribute paid to the "7th art" during the American film festival.

"Our collaboration with brasseries and bistros embraces various situations," explains Bruno Dubois, director of Maison Drucker. "It includes institutions located in Paris or Normandy that are familiar with our history, as well as interior design firms that work with us. But the work of some designers has also contributed to our success. Christian Biecher, for example, created an entirely original chair in 2007, for Café Fauchon on Place de la Madeleine in Paris, with a steel frame and sophisticated Rilsan weave, thereby representing the rattan of the twenty-first century. This creation, going against the grain of everything that had been done previously by Drucker, was produced in Java, because it was impossible to manufacture in France."

Worldwide, the Drucker chair flaunts its Parisian look, with its recognizable silhouette and caning evoking a jacquard weave, without ever clashing with the culture of its host country. It conveys part of our culture, our savoir-faire, even our exoticism, a bit like the pages of a history that has spread across the globe.

Café de Flore, Paris

6am, Rive Gauche!

The day rises on Saint-Germain-des-Prés. At *Café de Flore*, the waiters in their traditional long white aprons over black attire set the chairs out on the sidewalk. A couple of passing Japanese tourists wait patiently and attentively for the opening to enjoy an intoxicating first hot chocolate on the Paris street. Those two silhouettes reflecting in the window: Jean-Paul or Simone? Or maybe Juliette and Boris? No, the shadows are playing tricks. A legend goes by...

A circle of *Seine* chairs, armchairs, benches and stools.

Le Flore
Service Voiturier
face aux Deux Magots

RENDEZ-VOUS AU...
CAFE DE FLORE

Café Rey, Paris

7pm, Faubourg Saint-Antoine!

At the corner of Rue de la Roquette,
it's the moment for an aperitif. "What about
grabbing a drink in the sun at *Café Rey*?"
asks Marie-Hortense to her friend Edwige.
"These amusing chairs, with their Minnie Mouse
ears and their patriotic style, look very inviting...
Or how about at the bar: tasty sandwiches and
big glasses of red with Robert and Mimile?"

The friends have decided: the option "bistro
tradition" wins... *Paris Canaille* forever!

Standing to attention, *Parnasse* chairs in a
tricolor uniform.

The Patio of Prince de Galles, Paris

5pm, Avenue George V!

"It's lovely being on *The Patio of Prince de Galles.*
But where is Charles, my prince...? I'm waiting here! Very aesthetic, this Egyptian
mosaic colonnade... Twenty minutes late already, what a lout! All the same,
at the heart of Paris, this atrium has a winter garden feel, so intimate with its deep
armchairs, so romantic, in fact... Anyway, I'm now on my third *five o'clock tea,*
and still no prince in sight. That's enough, I'm leaving. Bye-bye Charles!"

Previous double page: the languorous curves of the Luxembourg armchair, produced in jade green; entrance to Hôtel Prince de Galles; in the Patio dotted with vegetation, the *Alésia* chair is also waiting... Below: on a mosaic background, the *Trèfle* armchair, and against the pedestal table, the *Bastille* armchair. Right page: a "couple" of *Trèfle* and *Luxembourg* armchairs at a table. Décor signed by the interior architect Bruno Borrione.

Café Français, Paris.

3pm, Place de la Bastille!

Beneath the foliage of the trees, it's terribly "in" to enjoy a little espresso on the terrace, on La Place... Opposite the *Opéra de la Bastille* and the *Génie de la Liberté* statue, a myriad of "bobos" (or "bourgeois bohemians," for those who don't know them yet...) have colonized the elegant chairs of the *Café Français*.

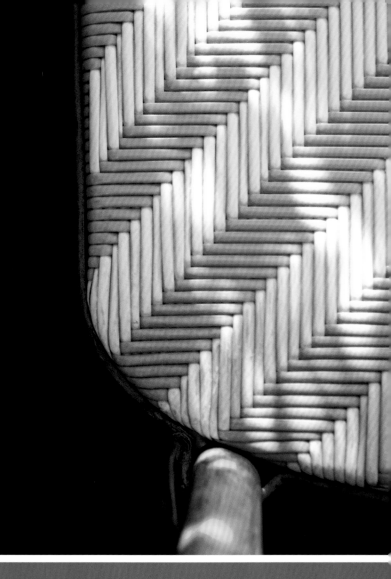

Noise, asphalt and drinks go well together.
But this location, designed by India Mahdavi,
is still so smart!

A flock of *Parnasse* chairs and stools with bicolor herringbone design.

Les Vapeurs, in Trouville

7am, Trouville!
At the crack of dawn, things are moving behind the bar: it's Denis, the *maître d'*,
at the helm for thirty years of this immutable ship, *Les Vapeurs!*
"The sixty chairs that run along the sidewalk must be perfectly aligned.
I want to see only one chair..." These seats have been welcoming famous
posteriors since 1927! A celebrated vintage, the restaurant is a top *cru*.
Between platters of seafood, it was the artist Savignac himself who illustrated
the menus of this legendary brasserie.

A flotilla of *Seine* chairs docked by the quay.

Moules
Frites
à toute heure

à Vin
itif

Restaurant du Perrey, in Étretat

1pm, Étretat!

It's full of excitement at *Restaurant du Perrey*: Monsieur Lupin, or Arsène to his friends, has reserved a front row overlooking the Aiguille, or the Needle as it is known in English. Always chic and seductive with his swirling black cape, he chooses a polychrome rattan seat. A seagull hovers above the Perrey, then plunges into the waves. A moment in suspension. On the gentleman thief's table, there remains only a monocle, the plate of mussels and... the bill! Our man has disappeared...

Beside the sea, a colorama of *Arc-en-ciel* chairs and benches.

On the boardwalk at Deauville…

Its beach, its boardwalk "Les Planches," and its cabins…
And also the Parisians enjoying the weekend, the Americans
appreciating the *French touch* and its movie stars!
This seaside annex of the capital, the twenty-first arrondissement of
Paris, fascinates with its glamour and its film references—
Clint Eastwood, Meryl Streep, Sean Connery and so many
others are immortalized in the famous "Bains Pompéiens."

Would that be Jean-Louis Trintignant and Anouk Aimé far off on
the beach? A remake of *Un homme et une femme*? No, the chairs
are empty, the canvas cabins folded up, the season is over…
Deauville, each fall, replays its film, and it's always a festival!

In shades of ocean blue, a trio of *Orléans*, *Saint-Michel* and *Parnasse* chairs.

Chez soi
in a Parisian Loft...

In the Kitchen

Are the high stools uniquely destined for various bar counters? Not at all! Taking up little space, they are equally at home in modern kitchens. Here, in a minimalist space that plays with immaculate white, they are a (red) highlight, a cherry on the cake (with icing). Three little uplifting notes as a counterpoint to the *Mur pour la Paix*, created by Clara Halter with Jean-Michel Wilmotte, that adorns the side of the lacquered glass bar.

In the Dining Room

Drucker chairs? Perfect for restaurants, cafés and terraces... Yes, of course, but not only that! These chairs so emblematic of the capital also know how to find their place in today's interiors. Here in a loft *à la mode* near Palais-Royal, for example. Formerly a carpet warehouse, it has been transformed into a private duplex by architect Marika Dru. A half-industrial, half-city spirit is preserved: a concrete floor and glass tiles, large atelier bay windows, and an original work by the famous American street artist, Toxic, *No Toys Allowed*, ruling over the scene. This graffiti piece, reproduced as a panoramic print, is now part of the collection of fabrics and wallpapers by Pierre Frey!

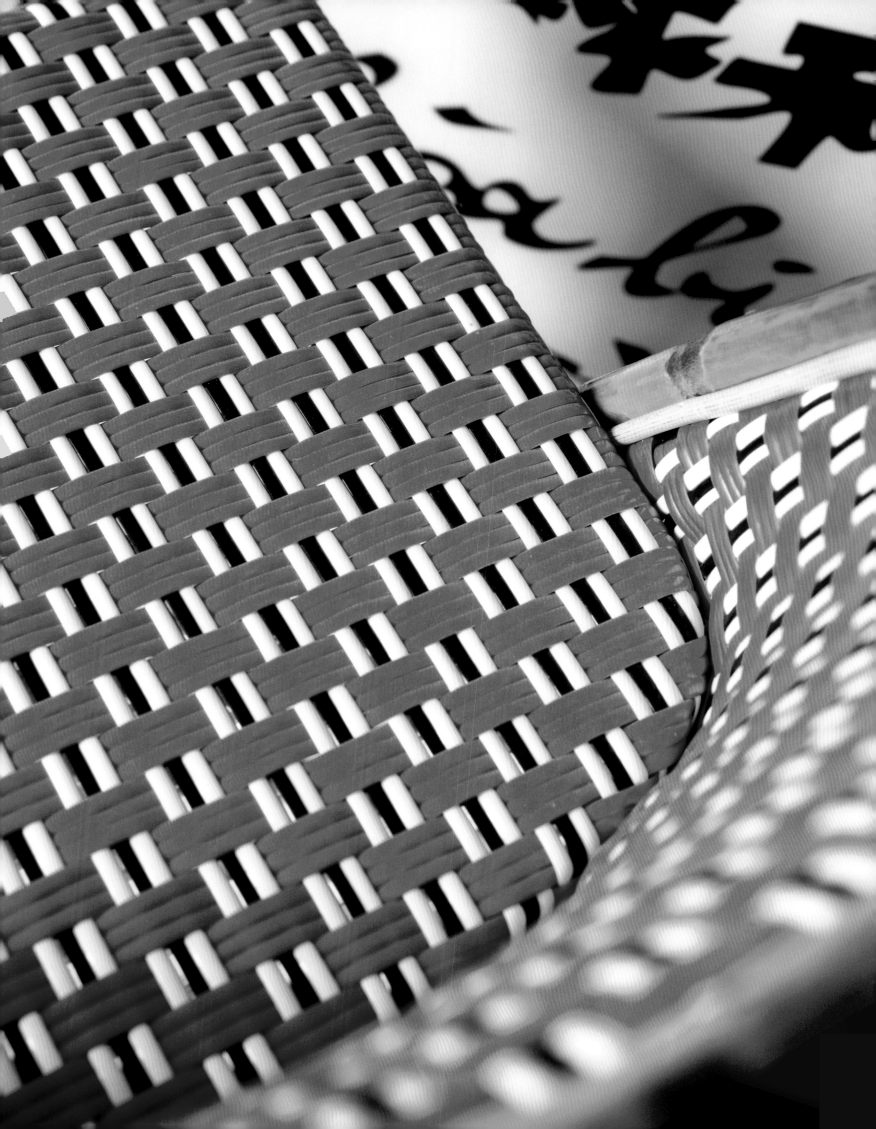

Right page: Matched and
mismatched, six chairs in sky colors:
from left to right, the *Matignon*,
*Sorbonne, Neuilly, Saint-Michel,
Bercy* and *Haussmann* chairs.
Previous page: In the kitchen,
bar stools, *Matignon* with solid back,
and *Fouquet's* with openwork,
and a standard version with cushion.

Contents

The International Influence of Drucker Aboard

In Europe

Paris Bistro, Baku (Azerbaïdjan)
Brasseries Georges, Brussels (Belgium)
Le Colonel, Saint-Gilles (Belgium)
Hôtel Métropole, Brussels (Belgium)
Café Europa, Copenhague (Danmark)
Café Bomhuset, Charlottenlund (Danmark)
Café Lumskebugten, Copenhague (Danmark)
Cote Restaurants, London (England)
Chiltern Street, hôtel à London (England)
The Wet Fish Cafe, à London (England)
Les Deux Salons, à London (England)
Paris Bar, Berlin (Germany)
Zarges, Frankfurt (Germany)
Palazzo Margherita Matera, Bernalda (MT) (Italy)
Monastero Santa Rosa, Conca dei Marini (Italy)
Café Cappuccino, Madrid and Palma de Majorque (Spain)
Crusto, Barcelona (Spain)
Café Kafka, Barcelona (Spain)
Restaurante Lateral, Madrid (Spain)
Brasserie Gerloczy, Budapest (Hungary)
Nordells Konditori, Arvika (Sweden)
Tures Brasserie & Bar, Stockholm (Sweden)
Rigoletto, Stockholm (Sweden)
Brasserie Godot, Stockholm (Sweden)
Kulturhuset, Stockholm (Sweden)
Restaurant Riche, Stockholm (Sweden)
Teatergrillen, Stockholm (Sweden)
Zink Grill, Stockholm (Sweden)
Storstad, Stockholm (Sweden)
M/S Gustavsberg (boat) (Sweden)
M/S Enköping (boat) (Sweden)
Kolben Kaffe Akademie, Freiburg (Switzerland)
Lake Geneva Heritage (boat) (Switzerland)
Hotel Les Trois Couronnes, Vevey (Switzerland)
Hotel Seegarten, Zurich (Switzerland)

In America

Bar Alexandre, Montréal (Canada)
Hôtel Mercure, Santiago (Chili)
Lima Marina Club, Lima (Péru)
Hôtel SLS, South Beach, Miami (United States)
Brasserie Marion, Miami (United States)
Le Zoo, Miami (United States)
Hôtel Chateau Marmont, Hollywood (United States)
Cafe Stella, Los Angeles (United States)
Parc Restaurant, Philadelphia (United States)
Le Diplomate, Washington (United States)
Christos Restaurante, New York (United States)
Sasha's Wine Bar, Clayton ((United States)
Virginia Inn Restaurant, Seattle (United States)
La Voile, Boston (United States)

Middle East

Fauchon (Koweit)
Café de Flore, Beiruth (Libanon)
Le Commodore Hôtel, Beiruth (Libanon)
Angelina, Beiruth (Libanon)
Les deux Magots (Qatar)
Fauchon, Dubaï (United Arab Emirates)

In Australia

Restaurant Mr. Wong, Sydney
Manly Wharf, Sydney
Coogee Pavilion, Coogee

In Asia

Brasserie Gavroche, Singapour

In Africa

Hôtel White Sands, Accra (Ghana)

Photography credits:

The photographs of this work were taken by Jean-Marc Palisse, with the exception of the Drucker archival documents graciously loaned by Alain Drucker (pages 17, 27, 28-29, 30-31, 34, 38, 46-47, 48, and 49).
Page 148, © Henri Cartier-Bresson/Magnum Photos.
Pages 184-185, ABLACK Torrick (dit TOXIC, C-One), No Toys Allowed, 2015,
Patrick Frey property, © Adagp, Paris, 2016.

Acknowledgements:

The Maison Drucker company would like to give special thanks to the following people for contributing to the creation of this book: Alix de Dives, Jean-Marc Palisse, Serge Gleizes, Laurence Maillet, Corinne Schmidt, Charlotte Court, all the team at Éditions de La Martinière who worked on it, India Mahdavi, Christian Biecher, François Champsaur, Jacques Grange, Patrick Gilles, Dorothée Boissier, Olivia Putman, Patrick Frey, Pierre and Vincent Frey, Madame Siljegovic, Thierry Coste, Frédérique Capelle, Bruno Borrione, Jérome Meslin, Philippe Sermoise, Pierre Léonforté, Alain Drucker and everyone working at Maison Drucker.

*Alix de Dives would like to thank all the staff at Maison Drucker.
From the administrative department to manufacturing and weaving,
everyone enthusiastically collaborated in the creation of this book.
Within it, they will find an echo of our gratitude.*

Photography : Jean-Marc Palisse
Authors : Alix de Dives, Serge Gleizes
Original French text translated by Trevor Eccles
Graphic design and artwork : Laurence Maillet

Distributed in 2017 by Abrams, an imprint of ABRAMS

© 2016, Published by Editions de La Martinière,
an Imprint of EDLM

Library of Congress Control Number: 2016931644

ISBN : 978-1-4197-2343-8

Color separation : APS Chromostyle
Printed and bound in Italy
10 9 8 7 6 5 4 3 2 1

THE ART OF BOOKS SINCE 1949

115 West 18th Street
New York, NY 10011
www.abramsbooks.com